The Romance of Emaré.

Early English Text Society.
Extra Series. No. XCIX.

1908 (for 1906; reprinted 1958).

PRICE 15s.

The Romance of Emaré.

RE-EDITED FROM THE MS.,
WITH INTRODUCTION, NOTES, AND GLOSSARY

BY

EDITH RICKERT, Ph.D.

Published for
THE EARLY ENGLISH TEXT SOCIETY
by the
OXFORD UNIVERSITY PRESS
LONDON NEW YORK TORONTO

KRAUS REPRINT
Millwood, N.Y.
1990

OXFORD
UNIVERSITY PRESS

Great Clarendon Street, Oxford OX2 6DP
United Kingdom

Oxford University Press is a department of the University of Oxford.
It furthers the University's objective of excellence in research, scholarship,
and education by publishing worldwide. Oxford is a registered trade mark of
Oxford University Press in the UK and in certain other countries

© The Early English Text Society 1908

The moral rights of the authors have been asserted

Database right Oxford University Press (maker)

First Edition published in 1908
Reprinted 1958

All rights reserved. No part of this publication may be reproduced,
stored in a retrieval system, or transmitted, in any form or by any means,
without the prior permission in writing of Oxford University Press,
or as expressly permitted by law, or under terms agreed with the appropriate
reprographics rights organization. Enquiries concerning reproduction
outside the scope of the above should be sent to the Rights Department,
Oxford University Press, at the address above

You must not circulate this book in any other form
and you must impose this same condition on any acquirer

Published in the United States of America by Oxford University Press
198 Madison Avenue, New York, NY 10016, United States of America

British Library Cataloguing in Publication Data
Data available

Library of Congress Cataloging in Publication Data
Data available

Extra Series, 99

ISBN 978-0-85-991703-2

PREFACE.

This edition was prepared in 1898–99; but as it had to wait its turn on the list of the Early English Text Society, it has been completely revised, and extended in the light of several fresh publications on the subject, which have appeared in the meantime. My thanks are due to Dr. Furnivall for good advice on many occasions, and to Professor Manly, of the University of Chicago, for reading the proofs.

London, July 19, 1907.

CONTENTS.

	PAGE
INTRODUCTION :—	
§ 1. MANUSCRIPT	ix
§ 2. EDITIONS	xi
§ 3. DIALECT	xiii
§ 4. METRE	xviii
§ 5. STYLE	xxii
§ 6. AUTHOR AND DATE	xxviii
§ 7. IMMEDIATE SOURCE	xxviii
§ 8. ORIGINS	xxxii
§ 9. CONCLUSION	xlviii
APPENDIX	xlix
TEXT	1
NOTES	33
GLOSSARIAL INDEX	49
INDEX OF NAMES	55

INTRODUCTION.

§ 1. *Manuscript*, pp. ix–xi.
§ 2. *Editions*, pp. xi–xiii.
§ 3. *Dialect*, pp. xiii–xviii.
§ 4. *Metre*, pp. xviii–xxii.
§ 5. *Style*, pp. xxii–xxvii.

§ 6. *Author and Date*, p. xxviii.
§ 7. *Immediate Source*, pp. xxviii–xxxii.
§ 8. *Origins*, pp. xxxii–xlvii.
§ 9. *Conclusion*, p. xlviii.

§ 1. THE MANUSCRIPT.

MS. Cotton Caligula A ii, in the British Museum, consists of two paper quartos, originally marked Vespasian D 8 and Vespasian D 21,[1] bound together with the present designation before 1654.[2]

Vespasian D 8, which contains *Emaré* (fols. 71–76) is, in the main, a collection of English verse (fols. 3–139);[3] Vespasian D 21 contains statutes of the Carthusian order, 1411–1504 (fols. 144–210); fols. 142, 143 seem to be the parchment cover of Vespasian D 21;[4] and fols. 1, 2, 140, 141, blank pages inserted when the two volumes were bound together.[5]

Vespasian D 21, in the 16th century, belonged to a Cambridgeshire family, the Cookes of Milton;[6] and very possibly came from Denney Abbey, about 7½ miles north of Cambridge.[7] The

---

[1] In a 17th century hand on fols. 3, 140.

[2] They are not mentioned in the two earliest catalogues extant; while in the third, compiled before 1654, Caligula A ii is entered with a table of contents corresponding to the *Elenchus* on fol. 1.

[3] Together with a translation from John of Bordeaux of a treatise on pestilence, and a form of confession in prose; also four prescriptions, and a short Latin chronicle.

[4] Fol. 143*b* contains the signature "Thomas Cooke gen)," which is plainly blotted on fol. 144*a*. Fol. 142 is blank and about ½ inch narrower than 143, as if it had been folded upon itself in the binding, in such a way that it brings the two rough sides of the parchment together.

[5] Fol. 1 contains the 17th century *Elenchus*. Fols. 1 and 2 show no water-marks, but the marks on fols. 140, 141 are different from all others in the book, and these folios are also shorter than the others, and with the lower edges untrimmed. In all four, the paper is thinner and of a different quality. In fols. 140, 141 the grain runs across, not down, the page.

[6] A second signature on fol. 143*b* is "Thomas Cooke de Mylton)." The writer was born in 1541, the elder son of Judge William Cooke, lord of the manor (see latter's will in Somerset House).

[7] At least, the Cookes seem to have built a new house out of its stones, when it was demolished in 1538 (*History of the Parish of Milton*, Camb. Antiq. Soc., XI, 1869, p. 28).

only clue to the origin of Vespasian D 8, the inscription "Donum Jo. Rogers" (fol. 3), in a 16th century hand, is too slight to be of use.[1]

Its date, however, can be ascertained within narrow limits. It contains Lydgate's *Nightingale* (fols. 59-64b), written not before 1446, almost certainly in that year;[2] likewise a short Latin chronicle of England (fols. 109-110), which is carried down to the reign of Henry VI by the hand that seems to have written all the other pieces[3] (except the four prescriptions on fol. 13b), while a second hand adds a note of Henry's death and the reign of Edward IV, and a third, the reign of Richard III. It is highly probable, then, that the bulk of the MS. was copied between 1446 and 1460.[4]

It shows a great mixture and confusion of forms:

1. Dentals.

(a) Interchange of d and th (= þ, ð) in all positions, as: þowȝtur, donder, dey; vnther, wordy (worthy), erdly; hondereth (hundred).

(b) Interchange of t and th (= þ) in all positions, as: thylle (tylle), tho (to); þowȝþur; knyȝth, whythe (white), etc.[5]

2. The inflectional and unaccented stem vowel. The proportions in *Emaré* alone, are as follows: -es 89, -ys 20, -us 18; -ur 97, -er 26, -yr 17; -ylle 18, -ulle 9, -elle 3.[6]

---

[1] Five men of that name, during the 16th century alone, are included in the *Dictionary of National Biography.*

[2] Lydgate's *Minor Poems*, ed. Glauning (E.E.T.S., Extra Series, LXXX), 1900, pp. xxxvii-xxxviii.

[3] This is not absolutely certain. The letters are formed similarly, but there is some variation in fineness and closeness. However, there is no abrupt break; and the gradual loosening of the hand, with occasional recurrences to closer writing, is better explained on the hypothesis of different times and moods than of different scribes.

[4] Cf. also Glauning, *op. cit.*, p. xi.

[5] This confusion in writing seems to mark a pronunciation in which the front of the tongue is pressed hard against the upper teeth, with an inevitable thickening of the dental sound. In Mid-Yorkshire such pronunciation is marked, affecting d initial and before a vowel, and initial and final t. Cf. C. Clough Robinson, *A Glossary of Words Pertaining to the Dialect of Mid-Yorkshire*, London, 1876, pp. xiv, xvii-xviii, and p. xv below. It is found extensively also in *Sir Gowther.*

[6] The -u seems to point to West Midland influence as the -y to Northern, and the -e to Southern. A peculiarity which may point to the home of the author or of the scribe is the use of gh to represent the sound th, as in sygh (= syth, 560), kygh (= kyth, 594). This survives to-day in the name of the town Keighley (pronounced Keithley) in the West Riding (cf. p. xvii below).

The Manuscript. Editions.

3. Partial palatalization of k : mykylle, mychylle; sykynge, worche, ylke, euerychone, etc.[1]

4. The insertion of inorganic ȝ or gh, as in kowȝþe, gryğht, etc.

The present MS., then, may be a Southern copy taken directly from a MS. written in the original dialect, including certain West Midland and Northern spellings by reason of proximity to these districts; but the irregularity and variety of the forms suggest rather that it has passed through several hands.

The MS. is incomplete, eight stanzas of *Sussan*, the first piece, being lost and a portion of the *Eustache*, which breaks off on fol. 139b.

Of the 139 leaves, about 93 contain romances or tales; 14½, three didactic poems by Lydgate; 26, short religious poems, chiefly lyrics;[2] and 5½ prose.

Of the twelve long narrative poems, eight are romances proper: (1) *Eglamour of Artas*, (2) *Octauian Imperator*,[3] (3) *Launfal Miles*,[3] (4) *Lybeaus Disconus*,[3] (5) *Emaré*, (6) *Sege of Ierusalem*, (7) *Cheuelere Assigne*, and (8) *Isumbras;* four are religious tales or romances: (9) *Sussan*, (10) *Ypotys*, (11) *Owayne Miles*, (12) *Tundale*.

From the plain workman-like character of the MS. and its marked religious and didactic element, it would seem to have been a tale book copied in some monastery.

§ 2. EDITIONS.

1. Ritson, *Ancient Engleish Metrical Romanceës*,[4] London, 1802, II, 204–247, with a list of original readings, III, 222, of corrections, III, 440, of conjectural emendations, III, 443, and full notes, III, 323–33. The text is practically correct, but does not indicate the graphic peculiarities of the MS.: þ is printed as th, medial and

---

[1] The partial palatalization might be accounted for by the passing of the MS. through the hands of several scribes; but it might also have belonged to the dialect.

[2] Three hortatory religious poems : *Carta Ihesu Christi*, *The Stacyonys of Rome*, *Trentale Sancti Gregorii;* two lives of saints, *Ierome* and *Eustache;* 14 religious lyrics.

[3] Thought by Sarrazin and Kaluza to be by the same author, Thomas Chestre, who certainly wrote *Launfal*. They are found together, as are also 6, 7, 8, and 10, 11, being separated from the other romances by religious matter. *Emaré* stands alone between a short prayer in verse and the *Carta Ihesu Christi*.

[4] Reprinted by Edmund Goldsmid, Edinburgh, 1885, with a few MS. readings, but also with fresh errors. Kölbing published a collation of Ritson with the MS., *Englische Studien*, XV, 248.

final ʒ as gh, initial ʒ as y; u and v, and i and y are not according to the MS.; the tail to n is disregarded except where I give the expansion in my notes, the tail to r always, and the crossing of ll and h; the contractions for ur, us, are printed er, es; contractions are expanded, and with the few exceptions given above, words joined or separated, and a few obvious corrections made, without indication of change.

2. Gough, *Emaré* (Morsbach and Holthausen, *Old and Middle English Texts*, vol. II), London, New York, Heidelberg, 1901. This text is normalized and considerably altered in an attempt to reconstruct the original, with MS. readings in the foot-notes, and a table on pp. x, xi of the principal classes of phonetic changes. Aside from these, in several points not deemed important enough for separate quotation, Dr. Gough's text differs from that of the present edition: the crossing of ll and h is disregarded, expanded contractions are sometimes differently italicized; the curl to r is sometimes disregarded, and again written r*e*; *w*, ñ is printed sometimes n sometimes *n*n, sometimes n*e*; u and v are not distinguished as in the MS.

The introduction is brief; but Dr. Gough treats of the sources of *Emaré* in his paper *On the Constance Saga* (Brandl and Schmidt, *Palaestra*, no. 23, Berlin, 1902) and its metrical and grammatical aspects in his dissertation, *On the Middle English Metrical Romance of Emaré*, Kiel, 1900, which I obtained late; hence, I have used it chiefly in my notes.

3. The present edition aims to give the text as the scribe intended it to be read. Expansions of contracted forms, additions and a few obvious corrections are indicated.[1] Capitals and punctuation are modern. It has been thought expedient to give in the foot-notes, aside from the classes of changes mentioned, the few special cases in which Ritson (R.) and Gough (G.) vary from the MS. Gough's emendations, in so far as they seem to find a basis in the text itself, are given in the notes at the end of the volume.

In a unique MS. which bears internal evidence of being a copy,[2] and shows a great mixture of dialects, I have not attempted to restore the text, believing that such a reconstruction must be largely arbitrary.

[1] Expansions by italics; additions in brackets; probable omissions in parentheses.
[2] Cf. *Emaré*, ll. 331, 332, 337, which show plainly that the scribe had lost his place; likewise 837, 839, 840.

I have departed from recent custom, in expanding ħ to lle inasmuch as in *Emaré* there is not a single instance of ll or ħe.[1] I have retained the marking of għ, ħ, w, ñ, r', because I am unable to find any principle governing the usage.

In regard to għ, ȝtħ, ħ, the balance of evidence seems to show that the stroke has lost its value, although in a few cases an -e added serves to correct the metre.[2]

The marking of m̄, ñ, w, if expanded at all, must be rendered sometimes un, nn, mm, sometimes me, ne; but there are also cases in which it must be meaningless.[3]

The curl to r seems to be mere ornament.[4]

In the *Introduction*, I have endeavoured, in addition to a brief treatment of the dialect and metre, which afford no special problems, to make a careful study of the style and sources of the poem, with a view to determining its place and relationships in mediaeval literature.

§ 3. DIALECT.

A. Phonology.

A study of the rhymes gives the following results:

a. Vowels.

O. E. ă is retained.[5]

O.E. ā wavers between o and a. It becomes o in fome (835, 818) rhyming with trone (836) and with come (817), trone (820), Rome (821); home (601) rhyming with sone (O.E. sōna, 602);

---

[1] The observation should have been continued throughout the MS. As far as I have been able to read (fully half), the exceptions to the rule are less than half-a-dozen, over against innumerable cases where the usage is uniform. I conclude that the sign still had meaning for this scribe.

[2] I have not observed these letters carefully throughout the MS. because in *Emaré* alone the irregularity is sufficiently great. In 63 cases, -ȝtħ, għ(t) lacks -e and requires none; in 42, it is required. In 16, -ȝth, -ȝh(t) lacks -e and requires none; in 4, it is required. In 3, -ȝhte occurs but the -e is unnecessary; in 3, it is needed. There are no cases of -ghte. These results are not final because in some cases lines may be read differently; but they serve to show the confusion of practice.

[3] In *Emaré*, gan occurs 10 times, gaw 3; vpow, vpoñ 7 times; vpone 1; home twice, hom 3 times, hom̄ once; none 3 times, now 4, non 4; etc. Altogether, I think much more evidence is desirable before trying to settle this point. In *Emaré*, the mark seems to be without meaning. Cf. also vsedew (62), louedew (124), seteñ (218), whēns (418), etc.

[4] In 91 cases in *Emaré*, we find -er, -ur; in 21 -ere; in 31 er'. Her as adverb occurs 19 times, here once, her' once; her as pronoun, 20 times, over against here once and her' 16 times. There is also a great preponderance of ther, þer, wer, neuur, euur, over the forms in -e.

[5] Cf. ll. 757–58; 1031–30; 195, 201.

anon) (886) with sone (O.E. sunu, 887); oon (157) with sonne (O.E. sunu, 158); lore (412) with be-fore (413). It is retained in gare (198) rhyming with chare (O.Fr. char, 201); sore (633) and more (636), with spare (630) and kare (O.E. cearu, 627); a-lone (693) and wo-by-gone (696) rhyming with name (O.E. nama, 687) and tane (690).

O.E. ă becomes usually a,[1] but twice e: was (463) rhyming with prese (O.Fr. presse, 464), sete (221, 893) with swete (O.E. swete, 220, 892).

O.E. ǣ becomes usually ‚e,[2] but it is once a: there (204) rhyming with chare (201) gare (O.E. gāra, 198) fare (O.E. faran, 195); and once o: wore (410) rhyming with be-fore (413).

O.E. ĕ remains[3] except in ecg, eg, where it becomes ay: say (416, 435) rhymes with ray (O.Fr. rai, 415) gay (O.Fr gai, 444).

O.E. ē remains.[4]

O.E. ĕā varies. It becomes a: bale 1010) rhyming with pale (O.Fr. pale, 1009); kare (627) with spare (O.E. spārian, 630). It becomes o: be-holde (249) rhyming with golde (O.E. gold, 243) and molde (O.E. molde, 246). It becomes e: marke (504) rhymes with clerke (O.E. cleric, O.Fr. clérc, 495).[5]

O.E. ēā becomes e,[6] once written ee: lees (O.E. lēas, 110) rhymes with heþennes (O.E. hæðennys, 109).

O.E. ĕō becomes e:[7] but ȝynge (380, etc.) rhymes with þyng (O.E. þing, 379–82) kyng (O.E. cyng, 383) etc.

O.E. ēō becomes e,[8] but both ȝede and ȝode occur: ȝede (O.E. ēōdon, 213) rhymes with stede (O.E. stĕda, 210); ȝode (O.E. ēōde, 516) with blode (O.E. blōd, 513) gode (O.E. gōd, 510), fode (O.E. fōda, 507).

O.E. ĭ, ī, ў, ȳ, from whatever source, remain as y, rhyming together and with French i.[9] The one exception is euylle (O.E. yfel, 535) rhyming with deuylle (536).[10]

---

[1] Cf. ll. 121-22, 289-90, 374-73, 459-62-65, 557-56, 773-72. So æg becomes ay : may (452) rhyming with ray (O.Fr. rai, 451).
[2] Cf. 207-210 ; 345-42-39 ; 826-27 ; 803-2 ; 662-61 ; 548-49-46-52 ; 1002-999.
[3] Cf. ll. 567-73-76 ; 190-91 ; 434-33.
[4] Cf. ll. 215-14 ; 237-34 ; 175-76 ; 342-39, etc.
[5] No other instances occur.   [6] Cf. ll.816-10-07.
[7] Cf. ll. 498-501-495.
[8] Cf. ll. 8-7, 423-26-32 ; 291-94-97-300 ; 792-89-86-83, etc.
[9] Cf. ll. 599-98 ; 327-30-33-36 ; 227-26 ; 951-54-57-60 ; 581-80 ; 526-27 etc.
[10] Also the e from y in heþennes (cf. ll. 109-10), but this was originally unstressed. Here (1005) probably came from the form heran.

Dialect. xv

O.E. ŏ remains.[1]

O.E. ō remains except before ʒth, ght where it becomes ow.[2]

O.E. ŭ becomes o.[3]

O E. ū becomes ow, rhyming with a similar development out of O.Fr. u, ou: towne (O.E. tūn, 804) rhymes with renowne (O.Fr. renumee, 801);[4] bowre (O.E. būr, 63) with flowre (O.Fr. flour, 66), honour (O.Fr. honour, 69), emperour (O.Fr. emperour, 72).[5]

b. Consonants.

The chief point of interest shown by the rhymes is that -h -gh, seems to have lost its guttural quality: hygh (O.E. higian, 103) rhymes with fayry (O.Fr. faerie, 104); hye (O.E. hēah, 193) with melodie, (O.Fr. melodie, 194).[6]

There is some evidence in ll. 663-66-69-72 to show that the author shared the scribe's confusion of d, th, (= þ, ð), or t, th (= þ) t.[7]

B. Inflections.

Inorganic -e is commonly written, but can rarely be attributed with any degree of certainty to the author.[8]

Nouns form their plural regularly in -s, -es (-is, -ys, -us in the MS.).[9] The plural in -n occurs once.[10] There are several plurals without ending,[11] one with umlaut.[12]

Adjectives have no ending or -e.

Pronouns are regular: me, we; þe, the, þyn; he.

Adverbs end in -ly, -lye, or have no ending.[13]

Verbs afford the chief tests of dialect.

---

[1] Cf. ll. 163-64, etc.   [2] Cf. ll. 2-1, 170-69, 583-84, etc.
[3] Cf. ll. 5-4, 224-25, 82-83, 978-75-81-84, etc.
[4] Also with treson, reson (795-98) which must stand for tresoun, resoun.
[5] Cf. also ll. 899-98; 663-66-72.   [6] Cl. also ll. 165-59-62-68.
[7] And perhaps (so G.), in the rhymes wrothe-othe (265-66), bot-wote (268-69).
[8] Cf. ll. 80, 349, 657, 694. Gough's emendations are given in the notes at the end. About a dozen other cases might be cited, all more or less uncertain.
[9] But sometimes two forms are used, as flowrys (29) and flour (125, 149); bowrys (28) and bowre (899). Plurals with and without -s often occur together (cf. ll. 91, 94, 154, 155, 389-90, 898-99).
[10] Yʒen (298) rhyming with syʒen (299).
[11] Honde (MS. hond*us*, 639) rhyming with londe (642), sonde (645) wronge (648); yere (816) rhymes with dere (813) clere (810) chere (807); ston (100) with non) (101); stye (196) with lady (197), strete (543) with swete (546), etc. þyng occurs frequently, but always in a formula probably archaic (cf. ll. 40, 64, etc.).
[12] Fete (211) rhymes with swete (212). Fote (1017) rhyming with bote (1011) I take to be a survival of the old dative plural fotum. Fete, however, is in the same construction.
[13] Cf. ll. 287-86; 631-32; 854-53; 868-69; 894-91-900-897.

The present infinitive loses its -n in 83 cases; and keeps it in 9, affecting, however, only 5 verbs: sene, done, bene, tane, gone.[1]

The present participle is not found in rhyme, the one case given by Wilda being inconclusive.[2]

The perfect participle keeps its -n in 9 cases, 5 verbs: done, sene, forlorne, borne, gone;[3] and loses it in 3 cases, 2 verbs: be, holde.[4]

The prefix y- is twice found and is necessary for the rhythm.[5]

The indicative present singular is not found. The plural ends in -e: (we) rede (216) rhymes with stede (210, dat. sing.); (ȝe) ryde (971) with be-tyde (970, 3rd sing. pres. opt.); (they) stonde (116) with honde (115, dat. sing.). Weak verbs have n + d become nt.[6]

Very few forms of the preterite occur.[7] Among strong verbs:[8] (she, he) sete (221, 893) rhyming with swete (220, 892); (they) ponge (659), with strong (658); (they) sye (68), sy (869), with slye (67), curteysly (868); and also (they) syȝen (299) rhyming with yȝen (298).

The optative ends in -e.[9]

The few preteritive present forms are not peculiar.[10]

Among the anomalous verbs, the only notable form is wes (written *was*) rhyming with prese (cf. p. xiv above).[11]

C. Summary.

The dialect is North-East Midland as Wilda[12] concluded; but its Northern character must be emphasized. Common to the

---

[1] Cf. ll. 423, 486–432, 483, 489, 492; 4, 975–5, 978, 981, 984; 426, 626–432, 625; 690–687–693–696; 741–35–738–744.

[2] *Über die Örtliche Verbreitung der Zwölfzeiligen Schweifreimstrophe in England*, Breslau, 1887, pp. 27, 28. The line is 974: "A-ȝeyn þe emperour komynge," where *komynge* is a verbal noun, of which there are various other instances (cf. ll. 118–119, 511, 759, etc., with a dependent genitive.

[3] Cf. ll. 229, 406, 469, 856–230, 407, 470, 857; 429–432; 255–261; 258, 520–264, 521; 696–693, 687.

[4] Cf. ll. 364, 718–365, 719; 1027–1028.

[5] Y-borne (520), y-dyȝth (395). In l. 440, which otherwise repeats l. 395, it is needed.

[6] Cf. ll. 235–36, 931–32, 190–91, etc.

[7] The old passive hätte appears as hyȝte (85), 3rd singular, but may be due to the scribe.

[8] Cf. ll. 235, 931, 1015–236, 932, 1016; 190, 434–191, 433, for weak verbs.

[9] Cf. ll. 263–62; 630–27; 253–54; 970–71.

[10] Cf. ll. 672–63–66–69; 269–68; 252–46–43; 720–17–14–11.

[11] The -s endings within the line (1032–1033) are more probably survivals than interpolations.

[12] *Op. cit.*, p. 26.

Dialect. xvii

Northern and Midland dialects are: (1) the wavering of O.E. ā between a and o;[1] (2) the retention of O.E. ȳ, ȳ (derived by umlaut);[2] (3) the adverbial ending -ly, -lye. Northern are: (1) the dropping of -n in the infinitive (the exceptions in *Emaré* occur in texts purely Northern); (2) the persistence of -n in the past participle; (3) the assimilation of the vowel of the plural to that of the singular, in the preterite of strong verbs.[3] On these grounds I judge that the author lived north of the Humber.

In the hope of obtaining additional evidence for or against this belief, I have compared the vocabulary of *Emaré* with more than 30 glossaries of the 14th and 15th centuries, and with the various modern word-lists published by the English Dialect Society. Among these last, the Yorkshire glossaries contain about 20 of the 40 uncommon or dialectical forms in *Emaré* (of which 10 or more are now obsolete), such as: bigging, ding, fell, felter, fra, gate (= way), gether, greet (= weep, with preterite gruot), kell, kith, lashed, lovesome, ma, mense, mickle, til (= to), wor, war (= was), yark. Of these 40 words,[4] Chaucer contains only 6;[5] of three Yorkshire texts, Y shows 28, T 23, MA 25;[6] three supposed Lancashire poems, EEAP, 25;[7] a text showing marks of both N.E.

---

[1] G. gives 17 cases of o to 3 of a. I count 15 o to 5 a, including *Abro* as determinative of o, which it certainly is not. Omitting *Abro*-rhymes, I make 9 o to 5 a; if Abro = Abra, as I have shown (note on l. 57 below), the count becomes 9 o to 11 a.

[2] Cf. also Kölbing's *Amis and Amiloun* (*Alteng. Bib.*, II), 1884, pp. xxxi-xxxii, in connection with ll. 109-10, 463-64.

[3] L. 659 only.

[4] After various experiments with different numbers of words, I decided to limit the comparison to those most characteristic and least common, barring words immediately derived from the French. Accordingly, I have used: byggynge, de[l]fulle, felle, feltred, fode, fryght (frith), gate (way), grette, kygh (kith), lasshed, lay (law), le, lufsumme, mangery, menske, molde, myn, mynge, rappes, sale, snelle, stye, þonge (donge), tylle, warye, ȝarked, ȝoo; and the forms: by-forn, drury, erdly, fro, gedered, kelle, keuered, moo, mykyl, tane, vmbraydest, word (world), ȝyng.

[5] Beforn, fro, keuered, lay, moo, tylle. That difference in scale of works compared does not obviate results appears thus: *Florence of Rome*, in 2187 lines, has 13 of these words, *Sir Gowther*, in 756, 19, to Chaucer's 6. *Promptorium Parvulorum* (Norfolk, circ. 1440) has 9, *Catholicon Anglicum* (N.E. Midland (?), 1483) has 12, or proportionately twice as many.

I must ask indulgence if here and there are errors in the counting, especially in the case of texts which lack glossaries; but an occasional mistake of this sort would not affect the general relationship of the groups of numbers.

[6] Y = *York Plays*, T = *Towneley Plays*, MA = Thornton *Morte Arthure* (supposed Yorkshire), all in MSS. nearly contemporary with Cotton Caligula A ii.

[7] *Early English Alliterative Poems* (ed. Morris, E. E. T. S. 1).

xviii   *Dialect. Metre.*

Midland and W. Midland dialects, WA, 30.[1] Further,[2] among about 40 modern English dialect lists, the Whitby and Mid-Yorkshire glossaries[3] contain each about 15 of these words, while those of N. W. Lincolnshire, the Lake District, Durham, Lancashire and Derby have from 7 to 12 each; and no list,[4] I believe, outside Yorkshire and its neighbours (as given above), shows more than 4. The dialect of *Emaré* thus belongs to the very locality indicated by Trivet (cf. p. xxxiii below), between the Humber and Knaresborough,[5] *i. e.* Mid-Yorkshire.

§ 4. METRE.

A. Stanza scheme.

Of the 86 12-line, tail-rhyme stanzas, 57 are according to the scheme: (1) aabccbddbeeb, or variants of this form; 29, according to (2) aabaabccbddb or variants.[6]

Among the 57, the modifications are entirely in the fourth unit of the stanza.[7] Thus we find: (*a*) aabccbddbeeb in 47 cases; (*b*) aabccbddbddb in 7 cases;[8] (*c*) aabccbddbccb in 2 cases;[9] (*d*) aabccbddbaab in one case.[10] That is, the last couplet may consist of (*a*) a fresh rhyme; (*b*) the third couplet repeated; (*c*) the second couplet repeated; (*d*) the first couplet repeated.

Among the 29, we find: (*a*) aabaabccbddb in 19 cases;[11]

---

[1] *Wars of Alexander* (early 15th century). Skeat (p. xxiii) points out the mixture of dialects, which seems to me to indicate a Border district.

[2] Among other texts, *Torrent of Portyngale, Degrevant, Isumbras* and *Eglamour* contain many of the words on the list; but the absence of complete glossaries makes comparison difficult.

[3] In general, the Mid-Yorkshire dialect is credited with being more "Scotch" than its neighbours (Robinson, *op. cit.* p. vii). I note that the so-called *Scottish Alliterative Poems* (ed. Amours, Sc. Text Soc.) contain 24 words in my list, and the *Destruction of Troy* (Scotch) has 18.

[4] See publications of the English Dialect Society.

[5] Robinson (*loc. cit.*). Trivet calls it *lieu mene* (p. 27) between England and Scotland. He was either unfamiliar with it, or considered London as the king's capital. But Knaresborough, although about midway between London and the Border, is not on either of the great roads to Scotland.

[6] For different counts, see below, p. xix, note 9.

[7] Except 86, which adds three lines: aabccbddbeebffb.

[8] Stanzas 27, 32, 51, 67, 70, 77, 83. Perhaps also 43, 47, but see p. xix below, with note 10.

[9] Stanzas 64, 71.   [10] Stanza 34.

[11] Stanzas 1, 3, 8, 12–13, 19, 28, 31, 39, 42, 46, 57–58, 60–63, 74–75, 79, 81. Thus there are three groups of two stanzas in succession. Possibly also 38, but see p. xx below, with note 10.

(b) aabaabccbccb in 7 cases;[1] (c) aabaabccbaab in 3 cases;[2] that is, the last couplet may repeat either of the others in its rhyme.

Emaré is unique among romances of this class in its mixture of stanza forms. Kölbing suggested that this was intentional,[3] and Wilda, in endorsing the view, added that the poem was perhaps first written in the stricter form, and afterwards altered by a scribe who had lost the feeling of the original.[4]

It does not seem probable, in this case, that so small a portion of the first rhyme-scheme would be preserved. The four romances constructed according to the stricter scheme show a very small degree of alteration.[5] Moreover, three of them are much older than *Emaré*,[6] and the fourth is in a different dialect.[7] It seems more probable that the poet, who shows but little originality in any way, wrote the 86 stanzas in the form that 57 have retained—a form which was popular in his dialect and time.[8]

Notwithstanding the large proportion[9] of stanzas in the stricter form, the greater variation in the couplets, according to both schemes, makes it practically certain that the minstrel's only concern was to have a fresh rhyme for his first and third couplets, leaving the second and fourth to repeat any of the others, as an additional grace of style, according to the conventional tags with which his memory was stored.[10]

---

[1] Stanzas 17, 26, 35, 59, 68–69, 82. This is Kölbing's Type II, found only in *Duke Rowlande and Sir Ottuell of Spayne*. I have not treated this separately, as it seems to me the personal idiosyncracy of an author who could hardly have influenced the writer of *Emaré*.

[2] Stanzas 9, 20, 78.

[3] *Op. cit.* pp. xix-xx.   [4] *Op. cit.* p. 27.

[5] According to Kölbing, (*op. cit.* pp. xv–xvii) *Amis and Amiloun* and the *Kyng of Tars* (in the Auchinleck MS.) show no exceptions. Reducing his numbers to terms of percentage I find that *Horn Childe and Maiden Rimnild* has 8½% of variation, *Lybeaus Disconus*, about 7%. If *Emaré* belonged here, the variation would be 66%.

[6] *Amis and Amiloun*, *Horn Childe*, *Kyng of Tars*.

[7] *Lybeaus Disconus*, in S.E. England.

[8] It is used in *Sir Gowther*, *Erl of Tolous*, *Torrent of Portyngale*; also, in *Isumbras*, *Eglamour*, *Athelston*, *Sir Cleges*, *Sege of Melayne*, *Le Bone Florence of Rome*.

[9] Nearly 34%. Kölbing gives 35 stanzas; Gough says "about 32," but includes 22, 23, 43, with imperfect rhymes not confirmed elsewhere. I count 29 without including the doubtful stanza 38. Using Kölbing's numbers for the other romances, I find the per cents of variation to be as follows : *Launfal*, 18½%; *Octavian*, 13%; *Isumbras* and the *Erl of Tolous*, 7%; *Rowland and Vernagu*, nearly 7%; *Athelston*, 5%; *Le Bone Florence of Rome*, 4½%; *Sir Amadas*, 4% and 3% (the versions printed by Robson and Weber respectively); *Sege of Melayne*, 2¼%; *Eglamour*, 2%; *Sir Cleges* and *Sir Gowther*, no variations (*op. cit.*, pp. xix-xx).

[10] With this accords the paucity of rhymes that he finds to make up his

B. RHYME.

The author's rhymes show the following peculiarities:

1. The accent is shifted to the ultima: (*a*) in French words rhyming together;[1] (*b*) in French words rhyming with English;[2] (*c*) in English words rhyming together.[3]
2. Assonance suffices: (*a*) m and n;[4] (*b*) nd and ng;[5] (*c*) d and t;[6] (*d*) t and k;[7] (*e*) f and þ.[8]
3. There is one clear case of imperfect vowel rhyme. Emaré[9] (1023) rhymes with he (1026) story (1029) Egarye (1032) glorye (1035). However the names should be spelled, y still rhymes with e in this instance.

The rhyme -ynge, -ende is doubtful. Stanza 7 (ll. 75–78–81–84) is possibly a patchwork of two (cf. p. xxxii, n. 5, below). If ll. 445–46 and 448–49 rhyme together, stanza 38 belongs to the stricter type, and ll. 510–11 and 514–15, ll. 559–60 and 562–63 rhyme together. I incline to think that this was the case, in that the assonance was admitted, alternative y and e forms existed for some of the words,[10] and later on, *e. g.* in Bale's *Kynge Johan* y and e rhymed together (cf. ll. 719, 879, 1198, 1970, 2208, 2238). But for another possibility, see note on l. 793.

---

stricter stanzas. Rhymes to none repeated in 6 stanzas; to þynge, in 5; þore and kny3t, in 4; grete, be, and honour, in 2 each; hye, day, ys, and woo are used once.

[1] Vanyte (105) Crystyante (108); emperour (25) towre (26), etc.

[2] Fayry (104) hygh (103); spycerye (853) hastylye (854), etc.

[3] Bygynnyng (16) kyng (17), gretlye (997) by (998); heþennes (109) lees (110); lady (197) stye (196), wommon (443) anon) (442), show an unstressed syllable rhyming with a stressed. Studyynge (283) sowenynge (284), rychely (517) hastyly (518), wommon (427) Crystendom (428), two unstressed syllables together.

[4] Nome (27) none (30). This occurs 14 times.

[5] Lond (664) stronge (665). Cf. also 639–42–45–48. It is possible that -ynke rhymes with -yng; spendyng (271, 592) drynke (272, 593); but the lines are short. Cf. note on ll. 271–72.

[6] Blede (552) lete (549), swete (546) strete (543).

[7] Loke (1014) bote (1011) fote (1017) sote (1020); gate (828) make (825) take (822) sake (819).

[8] Lyfe (222) wyfe (228) syþe (225) swyde (219).

[9] Emarye (840) fre (831) le (834) powste (837) suggest that the author intended Emare, the form usually found; Egare (360) ferly (351) lady (354) dye (357) suggest that he intended Egarye (found 704 rhyming with y, and 810 where Emare is meant) although Egare (*esgarec*) is the correct form. See p. xxix below.

[10] Notably, hynde, unhynde, wynde, fiend, viend, fynde; the other forms I do not know.

C. Rhythm.

The general effect, even allowing for corruptions of the text, is rough. Short lines can sometimes be rectified by the hypothesis of a lost -e; long lines, by omission of redundant or explanatory words or phrases. But there remain many verses that cannot be made to follow closely a strict iambic ideal.

These departures cannot be numbered accurately, inasmuch as there are often several ways of reading a line; but certain general principles of variation may be noted.

1. The first syllable of the first foot is lacking, the line beginning with a stress. This is true of about one-fourth of the total number of lines.[1]

Within the line there is no clear case that such an omission is warranted, although to avoid this conclusion it is sometimes necessary to emend where no obvious corruption exists.[2]

2. Instead of $x\acute{}$ we find $xx\acute{}$. I counted about 50 cases in the first foot, 17 in the last, 10 in the second, and 14 in the third. These numbers admit of considerable variation, but the principle holds that the practice is by far the most abundant in the first foot.[3]

3. There are also about a hundred cases[4] in which elision is necessary, or something like O.E. resolved stress prevails. As examples of the blurring or elision of vowels, may be given: In móny a dýuerse lónde (15), Syr Ártyus wás hys nóme (27); And spéke we of þe émperoúr (72);[5] of the tendency to run syllables together, especially in -yl, -en, -er (-ur, -yr), -ow, -eth: Wyth ménske and mýchyl honoúr (69); In héuen wyth hým þat wé may bé (11); Lórde, lette neúwr such sórow a-rýce (260); Now kómeth þe émperoúr of prýse (985).[6]

4. There are different arrangements of stresses. Occasionally the stressed syllable precedes the unstressed, as: Cértys, þys ýs a

---

[1] I counted 258 lines; but the number is more, rather than less.
[2] There are a few seeming instances of what Saintsbury calls "pause-feet" (*History of English Prosody*, London, 1906, I, 83); but most of these can easily be emended. Cf. ll. 184, 195, 200, 280, 433, 436, 453, 461, 495, 514, 691, 692, 715, 856.
[3] Where more than two unstressed syllables occur, the sense usually shows that the line is corrupt.
[4] I counted 94.
[5] Cf. ll. 81, 84, 86, 183, 310, 482, 596, etc.
[6] Cf. ll. 187, 208, 220, 230, 252, 322, 324, 335, 336, etc.

wýkked káse (647).¹ Again, we find x⌣́|⌣́x, a form which suggests a survival of the O.E. Type C, as: He hádde but oń chýld in hys lýue (43); In álle Crýstyanté (108); That dcéd shúlde she bé (267).²

In these data, appears the popular and English character of the poem, in contradistinction to the French classical influences of which it shows but little sign.

Aside from the general framework of the rhythm-scheme, I believe that the author worked largely by a metrical instinct in which the O.E. tradition survived, so that his ear was not offended by the free manipulation of stresses which the poem shows.³

§ 5. STYLE.

A. VOCABULARY.

The limitations of the author's vocabulary are best shown by a comparison with Gower's and Chaucer's versions of the same story. *Emaré* in 1035 lines uses 802 words; Gower in 1014 lines, 945 words; Chaucer in 1029 lines 1265 words—showing half again as large a vocabulary. The proportion of romance words in Chaucer is approximately 30%; in Gower, 26%; in *Emaré* only 19%.

These two facts bear out the popular origin of the poem.

Of adjectives, *Emaré* contains 88, 44% of these occurring only once, the highest number of repetitions of any one word being 40; Gower uses 58 adjectives, only 7% occurring but once, the highest number of repetitions being 15; Chaucer has 127 adjectives, 63% being found only once, and the highest number of repetitions being 21.

The difference in the character of the adjectives used is illuminating. Gower's words are the most colourless, being almost entirely concerned with the moral quality of the thing. Hence, he uses great, glad, false, good, and worthy most frequently, and his nearest approach to the concrete is: bare, bloody, pale, naked (ship). Chaucer shows more appeal to the senses, as in: cold, dry, salt, bitter (figurative), pale, bloody, sheen, dark (figurative); and to the emotions, as in: woful, fatal, wretched, tender, cruel,

---

¹ I noted a number of cases that might be so read, but in many of them the accent of the word is uncertain, or the line admits of scansion in another way. Cf. however ll. 31, 104, 168, 261, 413, 415, 488, 605, etc.

² Cf. ll. 43, 47, 112, 156, 186, 201, 233, 294, etc.

³ This, as far as it goes, accords with Saintsbury's doctrine of English rhythm (*loc. cit.*).

Style. Alliteration.

cursed, weary, etc. In *Emaré*, while most of the adjectives occur repeatedly in all the 6- and 12-line stanza romances,[1] there is rather more sense-appeal than in Chaucer, but much less appeal to the emotions. For example we find: white, blue (meaning dark), gold, azure,[2] bright, sheen, pale, wan, clear, glistering, salt, delicious, cold, silken; but of words appealing immediately to the emotions nothing stronger than: lovesome.

Of adverbs, *Emaré* has 28, Gower 17, and Chaucer 32. Here again the same differences appear. It is rather curious that in all three, words showing speed should be most used: Gower has: suddenly (6 times); fast (4); Chaucer: shortly (6); *Emaré:* hastily (5). Aside from these, Gower shows the same dryness and Chaucer the same emotional appeal; *Emaré* is less rich in adverbs than in adjectives. Among those most used are: courteously, sweetly (swete, sote), specially and veramant.

Emaré is singularly bare of figures, containing only seven similes: white as whale's bone, as lily-flower, as flower, as flower on hill, as foam; bright as summer's day; lean as a tree; and two cases of synecdoche: salt foam for sea, white chin for beautiful face.[3]

B. ALLITERATION.

Alliteration in *Emaré* is an important device of style. It is found in about 200 lines, two words usually being so connected, but occasionally three[4] and even four.[5]

To a less noticeable extent, alliteration serves to connect two lines, two,[6] three,[7] even four words[8] being so used.

Where the alliteration passes beyond the limits of the line, the words do not seem to stand in any definite relationship to one

---

[1] Such as great (40 times), fair (39), rich (17), bright (14), fre (13), noble, seemly, sweet (each 12), etc.

[2] L. 113. Gold refers also to the material, and perhaps azure means *lapis lazuli*. The whole passage (ll. 88-168) containing the list of precious stones, is full of colour, but the effect is due to the nouns.

[3] Ll. 33, 66, 205; 946, 729; 818; 192, 438; 365; 835; 924.

[4] In 11 cases.   [5] In l. 29 only.

[6] Especially ll. 340-41-42, 376-77, 427-28, 487-88, 541-42, 833-34, 848-49, 923-24, 1010-11. I counted about 40 possible cases in all; but in many the effect was so slight that it may well have been accidental.

[7] Cf. ll. 83-84, 218-19, 314-15, 365-66, 497-98, 572-73, 611-12, 646-47, 737-38, 779-80.

[8] Cf. ll. 20-21, 170-71, 193-94, 227-28, 604-5, 647-48, 766-67, 887-88. Here nearly all the chief words alliterate. In ll. 586-88, three alliterative letters are spread over three lines; but it is difficult to say how far this was a conscious device of style.

another; within the line, their connections may be classified as follows:

(1) Noun and adjective:[1] And gode garnettes by-twene (156).

(2) Adjective with (a) chief or (b) secondary word of modifying phrase:[2] (a) Was godely vnþur gare (198); (b) Whyte as whales bone (33).

(3) Two words (a) nouns, (b) adjectives, or (c) verbs in the same construction:[3] (a) That made both see *and* sonde (18); (b) Of a lady fayr *and* fre (22); (c) And alle þat shalle dele *and* dyghte (3).

(4) Verb with (a) chief, (b) secondary word of modifying phrase:[4] (a) As I here synge in songe (24); (b) Wyth sory herte she songe hyt a-slepe (662).

(5) Verb with noun as (a) subject, (b) object:[5] (a) The kynges loue on her was lent (404); (b) And ledde hys lyf yn weddewede (77).

(6) Verb and adverb:[6] Such sorow was here ȝarked ȝore (329).

(7) Noun with (a) chief or (b) secondary word of modifying phrase:[7] (a) Thorow þe grace of God yn trone (680): (b) In þat robe of ryche ble (644).

(8) Nouns directly modifying another noun:[8] Of Babylone þe sowdan sonne (158).

(9) Noun with chief word of dependent clause:[9] The stones þat yn þys cloth stonde (116).

(10) Verb with predicate adjective: He wax alle pale *and* wanne (771).[10]

(11) Words not related directly:[11] And myȝte not fynde þat lady fre (308).

From this analysis it appears that alliteration is a vital and fundamental part of the author's mode of thought; and that as it is used to connect words in almost every conceivable relation in the

---

[1] 37 cases.
[2] 29 with chief word; 8 with secondary; 37 altogether.
[3] 14 cases of nouns; 8 of adjectives; 7 of verbs; 29 altogether.
[4] 18 with chief word; 1 with secondary; 19 in all.
[5] 6 times as subject; 17 as object; once with a predicate adjective; 24 in all. [6] 15 times.
[7] 12 times with chief; 2 with secondary; 14 in all.
[8] 11 cases.   [9] 8 cases.   [10] No other case.
[11] Only 5 other cases where the alliterative effect is unmistakable. As: Þe worde shulde sprynge fer and wyde (256). And she s(h)ewed sylke werke yn bour (730). He was resseuyed *and* rychely dyȝt (578). The lady *and* þe lytylle chylde (649). Wyth menske *and* mychyl honour (69).

sentence, it thereby maintains its place as the more natural element in the language, upon which the rhyme-scheme has been imposed.

Looked at from the point of view of content, the greater part of these alliterative expressions consists of the conventional phrases used repeatedly in all the 6- and 12-line stanza romances. In a few cases the expressions are peculiar to *Emaré*, while there are perhaps 50 more conventional lines, not in their present form alliterative. This number must be slightly reduced, in that some of these lines have alliterative equivalents from which they may have been derived.[1] But, on the whole, the alliterative expressions represent the bulk of the conventionalisms, as no doubt it was the alliterative connection that attached them to the memory.

As to character and content,[2] the alliterative expressions may be classified according to (*a*) participation in the same idea, *i. e.* derivation from the same root:[3] As I here synge in songe (24); (*b*) extension or qualification, *i. e.* further definition of the same idea:[4] That semely ys of syght (9); (*c*) association of like ideas:[5] Bothe by stye and strete (543); (*d*) differentiation, by association, of contrasting ideas:[6] Bothe yn wo and wele (573).

The fifty lines or thereabouts which are conventional in character but cannot be traced to an alliterative origin, may be classified as follows:

(*a*) References to source;[7] (*b*) assurances of truth:[8] In trwe story as y say (544); (*c*) strengthening of previous assertion: (1) by denying the contrary:[9] With-oute ony lettynge (843); (2) by repetition in different terms:[10] Men calle hyt heuen lyghte (6); (3) by further detail:[11] In alle maner of thynge (75); (*d*) allusions to God's will:[12] As hyt was Goddys wylle (327); (*e*) statement of time:[13] On þe morn when hyt was day (541); (*f*) a passing

---

[1] As: Semely to be-holde (sene), 942; wepte (grette) and ʒaf hem ylle, 778; flesh and bone (fell), 735; "wesh and seten don (wenten) to mete, 218."

[2] Kölbing's divisions (*Amis and Amiloun*, pp. lxvi-lxx) do not seem mutually exclusive; so I have preferred to classify separately according to structure and to idea.

[3] Rare. Cf. ll. 405, 465.

[4] Very common. Cf. ll. 96, 153, 198, 216, 246, 303, 366, 507, etc.

[5] Fairly common. Cf. ll. 3, 42, 174, 228, 474, 495, 600, 804.

[6] Rare. Cf. l. 18.

[7] In *Emaré* usually alliterative. Cf. ll. 216, 405. Ll. 162, 1029 are conventional in French rather than in English.

[8] Elsewhere alliterative. Cf. ll. 396, 144, 153, 381.   [9] No other instance.

[10] Cf. ll. 30, 36, 111.   [11] Cf. ll. 51, 108, 123, etc.

[12] Cf. ll. 450, 480, 675.   [13] No other examples in *Emaré*.

description of a character:[1] He was curtays in all*e* þyng¹ (40); (*g*) a customary gesture:[2] And sette hym on hys kne (87); (*h*) a customary act: Messengeres forth he sent³ (190); (*i*) expressions of sympathy:[4] And þat was gret pyte (276); (*j*) strongly associated ideas:[5] In halle ny yn bowres (873); (*k*) strongly contrasted ideas:[6] Bothe to olde *and* to ȝynge (41); (*l*) figures of speech:[7] And whythe as lylye flowre (66).

It appears at once that these do not belong to the story, but essentially to the machinery of the poem.

C. REPETITION.

Emaré is peculiar, even among romances of its class, for the large proportion of repetitions that it contains. Whenever the idea recurs the phrase, line, sentence, stanza, or even group of stanzas, is repeated, with only slight necessary changes.

It is interesting to note that among lines which almost exactly repeat others: 45 are used twice; 10, three times;[8] 2, four times;[9] 1 is used five times;[10] one six times.[11] This makes a total of 80 lines copied after 59 others. Among approximate repetitions: 52 are used twice; 14, three times;[12] 3, four times;[13] 1 is used five times.[14] This total is of 93 lines based on 70 others.

It appears, then, that 173 lines, or about $16\frac{1}{2}\%$ of the poem, could be omitted almost without reduction of vocabulary.

Further, whole passages describing similar episodes show strong resemblance in structure and phrasing. Such descriptions are:
1. The four corners of the cloth.[15]
2. Love at first sight.[16]
3. Lamentation (four times).[17]
4. Experiences in the boat.[18]

---

[1] Cf. ll. 30, 36, 39, 45, 64, 379, 513, 724.   [2] Cf. ll. 778, 893.
[3] Cf. ll. 180, 1027.   [4] Cf. ll. 336, 648, 684.
[5] Cf. ll. 300, 384, 390.   [6] Cf. ll. 65, 462, 571, 666, 863, etc.
[7] Cf. ll. 192, 205, 729.
[8] Cf. ll. 9, 48, 171; 217, 865, 889; 325, 673, 721, etc.
[9] Ll. 40, 64, 379, 724; 41, 64, 380, 725.
[10] Ll. 290, 556, 604, 646, 772.   [11] Ll. 93, 135, 141, 423, 471, 486.
[12] Cf. ll. 3, 42, 826; 204, 937, 1021; 331, 337, 679; 336, 648, 684, etc.
[13] Cf. ll. 555, 763, 882, 925; 28, 755, 873, 899; 207, 363, 453, 708.
[14] Ll. 250, 366, 612, 736, 988.
[15] Cf. ll. 121–32; 133–44; 145–56; 157–68.   [16] Ll. 220–31; 397–408.
[17] Ll. 280–300; 547–64; 604–12; 769–83.
[18] Ll. 313–24 and 325–36; 649–60 and 673–84.

5. The rescue by Kadore and by Iurdan.[1]
6. The messenger's reception (twice) by the old queen.[2]
7. The King's resolve to do penance and the Emperor's.[3]
8. Segramour's instructions upon the coming of the King and of the Emperor.[4]
9. The rejoicing over Emaré's restoration to her husband and to her father.[5]

The double structure of the poem accounts for a certain amount of parallelism; but this is so much greater than in any other version, that I judge the author to have had no close acquaintance with his original; but to have known this only in general outline and to have been thrown upon his own resources for details.

D. Sentence Structure.

The sentence structure and phrasing are uncommonly rough and careless, and no doubt often corrupted in transmission. The paratactic sentence prevails throughout, only the simplest clauses of time, place and comparison being subordinated.[6] When transitional expressions are found, they are crude and abrupt.[7] As in the ballads, speeches are introduced without mention of the speaker;[8] and indirect discourse is changed to direct in the same passage, without indication.[9] The subject is very often repeated in different forms, in a manner suggesting the progression of an Old English sentence;[10] while, on the other hand, it is omitted in lists of verbs where it is needed.[11] The connection is extremely loose, *that* being often omitted;[12] and sentences are regularly made up of several short clauses with different subjects.[13] A few special grammatical peculiarities will be given in the notes. Here again the character of a popular poem by a market-place minstrel is maintained.

[1] Ll. 340-84; 685-732.　　[2] Ll. 514-17 and 525-35; 574-86.
[3] Ll. 817-28; 949-960.
[4] Ll. 904-09 and 916-24; 973-84; 991-96; 1009-20.
[5] Ll. 625-36; 1009-20.
[6] The pronouns *who* and *which* are not found at all.
[7] Usually: Now leue we . . . and speke we, or its equivalent. Cf. ll. 70-72, 310-12, 742-44, 946-47.
[8] Cf. ll. 172-77.　　[9] Cf. ll. 520-22; 595-97; 715-20; 820-22.
[10] Ll. 52-53, 85-86, etc.
[11] Ll. 201, 271-73, 451-53; 763-64, etc.
[12] Ll. 232, 394-96, 403-4 etc.　　[13] Cf. ll. 328-36, 502-4, etc.

xxviii   *Author and Date. Immediate Source.*

§ 6. AUTHOR AND DATE.

The terminus *ad quem* for the date is 1446; *a quo*, 1350, inasmuch as the -e as a factor in the verse has almost disappeared.[1] The absence of archaic forms suggests a post-Chaucerian date; and 1400 is probably nearer the fact than is 1350.

The author was neither courtly nor learned, but was doubtless a wandering minstrel, who sang in the market-place.[2] He seems to have been a Yorkshireman, perhaps of the moor district, working up a local legend, in part, however, derived from a French, hence not popular, source.

§ 7. IMMEDIATE SOURCE.

Emaré is one of seven Middle English poems[3] that claim derivation from a lay of Britain. In two cases, *Lai le Freine* and *Launfal*, the original is extant, while the general agreement in character of the seven, renders it probable that all had similar sources. All are short (500–1200 lines), correspond to the description of a lay in *Sir Orfeo*,[4] and in form are suited to musical accompaniment.[5]

In the case of *Emaré*, the evidence for a French original, whether lay or romance, is considerable.

1. The names are French: Cesyle, Cysyle; Galys;[6] Artyus;[7] Dame Erayne;[8] Segramour, Segramowre;[9] Kadore;[10] Iurdan;[11]

---

[1] It is negligible in the proportion of three to one; and is occasionally inorganic.

[2] Instead of the usual references to listeners in the hall, we have l. 19, with its possible implication of the idea of a moving throng.

[3] *Sir Orfeo* (ll. 1–22), *Lai le Freine* (ll. 1–26), *Sir Gowther* (ll. 28–29, 751, 753), *The Erl of Tolous* (ll. 1219–21); *Launfal* (ll. 4–5), the only case in which Britain is not specified; Chaucer's *Franklin's Tale* (ll. 709–15) and *Emaré* (ll. 1030–32).   [4] Ll. 1–22.

[5] Cf. *Emaré*, ll. 24, 319; *Guigemar* (ll. 885–86), *Chievrefoil* (ll. 112–13) by Marie de France; *Le Lai de L'Épervier* (ll. 230–32, *Romania*, 1878, p. 9), *Doon* (ll. 1–4, 287–88, *Romania*, 1879, pp. 61, 64).

[6] For Gales or Galice? See note on l. 338 below. Both forms are French.

[7] Artus is the common form in French. In *Ipomedon*, one scribe writes Artus for Atreus (cf. Ward, *Catalogue of Romances*, I, 732); but here Arthur is clearly meant.

[8] Igrayne or Elayne? Both French.

[9] Cf. especially *Perceval le Gallois* (5598 ff., 13944); *Erec et Enide* (1733, 2231, 2238, 2250), Beaujeu's *Li Biaus Desconneus* (879, 5905, 6020); Malory's *Morte Arthur* (ed. Somer, List of Names); Froissart's *Méliador* (ed. Longnon, Index); *Claris et Laris* (ed. Alton, Index). The lost German romance, *Saigremor*, was seemingly based upon a French original.

[10] The equivalent in French romances of the Celtic Cadoc (F. Lot, *Romania*, xxx, 11–13). It occurs in *Perceval* (12964 ff.); in *Erec* (4515, 4545, 4574); in *Li Biaus Desconneus* as Cadoc (5694, 5702, 5708). Cf. also *Geoffrey of*

Tergaunte;[1] Abro;[2] Ydoyne and Amadas;[3] Florys and Blawncheflour;[4] Trystram and Isowde;[5] Emaré; Egaré.

2. The form Segramowres (876) rhyming with kowrs (867) honowres (870) bowres (873) is an old French nominative singular. The direct quotation may have been taken literally from the original.

3. The names Emaré, Egaré, clearly indicate a French source. Emaré seems to stand for *Emarie* (Emarye occurs once)[6] from French *esmarie* (afflicted, troubled); Egaré is from the French *esgarée* (outcast).[7] But I cannot think that the English poet intended to use *emarie* in the sense given. Usually the word is associated with *esgarée*, while here a contrast, if anything, is indicated.[8] The name which I believe the minstrel had in mind is Emeré,[9] which occurs as *La Blonde Esmeree*, in *Li Biaus Desconneus*.[10] This means pure, refined (as gold), endowed with rare qualities.[12] The *e* might easily have become *a* by analogy to Egaré with which Emaré frequently rhymes.

Monmouth, Layamon, the Thornton *Morte Arthure*, *Claris et Laris*, *Anseïs de Cartage*, etc.

[11] The hero of the French romance *Jourdains de Blaivies*. It occurs in *Geoffrey of Monmouth*, in the Huth *Merlin* and in *Malory*. (See p. xxxvii, note 6.)

[1] See note on l. 85 below. The name is certainly of French origin.

[2] Abra occurs in *Amadis of Greece* (Part II, ch. 1), of which the earliest extant form is French. On the ultimate origin of the word, see note on l. 57 below.

[3] The chief characters of a French romance of which no English version is known, although they are repeatedly mentioned in English books.

[4] The chief characters of a widely popular French romance.

[5] The spelling is much as in the Northern *Sir Tristrem*, the *Cursor Mundi*, and in *Malory*; but the oldest extant form of the story is French.

[6] L. 840, but the rhymes are: fre, le, powste. However, in ll. 1023, 1032, Emaré and Egarye rhyme with he, storye, glorye; and in ll. 1006-7, they rhyme together; hence the poet knew no distinction of an original *e*, *ie*. See p. xx above.

[7] Cf. Suchier, *Oeuvres de Beaumanoir* (Soc. des. Anc. Tex. Fr.), 1884, p. xlv.

[8] Cf. ll. 22-23, 47-48, 50-51. Such a contrast is suggested in the *chanson de geste*, *Herpin de Bourges*, based upon another version of this same story, in which the heroine Joyeuse calls herself Tristouse during her exile (Suchier, *op. cit.*, p. lxxxiii). Both words are so common that it is perhaps unnecessary to give instances of their use. Among Godefroi's quotations is: "Triste et dolente et esmarie." The word *esgarée* is found especially in romances of this group as *La Manekine*, *La Belle Hélène de Constantinople*, *La Comtesse d'Anjou*, also in *Berte as Grans Piés*; and there seems little doubt that the poet took it directly from his original. See also note on l. 1032 below.

[9] This occurs as a man's name in *Le Bone Florence of Rome*; but is pronounced *Emère*, rhyming with *clere*, *dere*, etc. The French *Esmeré(s)* is found in *Aucassin et Nicolete*, *Bauduin de Sebourc*, *Mainet* (Gautier, *Les Épopées Françaises*, Paris, 1869, III, 38), and elsewhere.

[10] Ll. 3638, 3804, 3842, 4963, 5466, 5793, 6002, 6053, 6066.

[12] According to Godefroi.

4. Probably the title of the source is indicated in ll. 1030-32:

"Thys ys on of Brytayne layes,
That was vsed by olde dayes,
Men callys 'playn þe garye.'"

The last line is clearly corrupt. Emendations[1] that suggest themselves are: "*Playn*[*t*] *d'Egarye*" (cf. l. 314), or "*Playnt Egarye*."[2] Whether *playnt* has become substituted for the usual *lai*, through misunderstanding of the character of this kind of composition, or has actually been transferred from a lyric on the theme that existed in the time of the *lai* and the various romances, is a point for conjecture.[3]

5. Without laying too much stress on the curious rather than numerous words of French origin,[4] we may note a few among them which suggest direct transference, such as: *acyse, crapawtes, perydotes*, possibly *fayry* (in the sense of fairy-work) and *vanyte*, the forms *testymonyeth* and *Segramowres;* and perhaps the phrases *a-fyne* and *cler of vyce*.

Altogether, there can be little doubt that the immediate source of the minstrel was French. A further question is, whether the English version is a more or less close rendering, which would probably be the case if it was a lay, or a condensation and retelling in outline, of the story, which would have been necessary if the author had worked upon the basis of a romance.

The French version must have been anterior to *La Manekine* and the original of *Mai und Beaflor* and Enikel's *Weltbuch;* hence cannot be later than the first half of the thirteenth century. That it is not older than this date appears, if in no other way, by the passage concerning the robe (82–180). That this was in the original is clear not only from allusions to it in several early versions;[5] but

---

[1] Suchier translates "On l'appelle simplement la Garie (ou l'Egarée?)"; but the definite article is not so used in English (*op. cit.*, p. xlv).

[2] On the interchange of d and th, þ, and t, th, cf. p. x above. Ten Brink derives the name Degarre from d'Egaré (ed. Brandl, 1899, p. 293). If this holds, the word must have come from some title containing *de*, perhaps *Lai d'Egarré* (so Degrevant from Agravain or Egrevain).

[3] *Emaré* is not a *plaint* or *complaint* (although "der Büheler" calls it a *clegliche mer, Die Königstochter von Frankreich*, ll. 1769, 1553, etc.). But this form, in the 13th century, was popular in French, and in the 14th was made fashionable in England by Chaucer and his school. In this connection, it is interesting to observe that the so-called "*Wife's Complaint*" in its matter is exactly a "Playn[t] d'*Egarye*."

[4] About 25% of the words in the glossary; 19% of the entire number.

[5] Notably in *La Manekine, Enikel, La Comtesse d'Anjou* and *Historia del Rey de Hungria*, although it is mentioned in many.

Immediate Source.

especially from a comparison between *Emaré* and *Mai und Beaflor:*

"ein samît lâȝûrblâ	(cf. *Em*, ryche golde and asowr, l. 113).
verre brâht ûȝ Persîâ	(cf. *Em*, 109, 116–17).
der was schône gehêret	
grôȝ vlîȝ dar an gekêret	(cf. *Em*, 118–19).
von meisterlîchen handen.	(cf. *Em*, 111).
eȝ wurden in allen landen	
nie gesehen sô richiu kleit,	(cf. *Em*, 107–8).
. . . . . .	
dar obe ein rîcher mandel	
geworht von tiurer koste.	
manec edel stein drûf gloste,	(cf. *Em*, 89–90, 110–1).
die hôher kraft niht wâren vrî.	
edele borton von Arâbî," etc.	(col. 40, ll. 29–35 and col. 41, ll. 1–4).

The "samît lâȝûrblâ" from Persia and the "golde and asowr" from Babylon must refer to the same cloth. A suggestion as to the date of the French original lies in the detail not found elsewhere that it was a gift to the Emperor Artyus from the King of Sicily. As the description seems to refer to a particular robe, the allusion to its origin is probably not without basis.[1] In 1191, Richard Cœur de Lion in Sicily was visited by Tancred, king of that country, and presented with many magnificent gifts, including *pannis sericis*.[2] That these were of Saracen work seems almost certain, in that the Mussulman weaving and embroidery, always famous, had received a great impulse under the Norman Kings during the twelfth century.[3] As the tale of the demonic wife was early attached to the legend of Richard Cœur de Lion,[4] an allusion to Tancred[5] is not so amazing as it seems. According to Philippe

---

[1] Moreover, the cloths made in Palermo answer to the description in *Emaré* (88–168): "tessuti con bell'artifizio a figure di animale e di piante, rilevati ad oro ed a colori diversi." On figures and portraits, cf. Michel, *Recherches sur le Commerce, la Fabrication et l'Usage des Étoffes de Soie, d'Or, et d'Argent*, Paris, 1852–54, especially II, 354–55.

[2] Related by the contemporary chronicler known as Benedict of Peterborough (Rolls Series), 1867, II, 159.

[3] Cf. Amari, *Storia dei Musulmani in Sicilia*, Firenze, 1854–72, III, 800–1, and Michel, *op. cit.*, I, 73 f.

[4] The English romance (*circ.* 1300), a translation from a lost French poem, represents her as coming in a magic ship (cf. the tale of the second Offa).

[5] *Tergaunte* from *Tancred* is as possible as many other confusions that are known to have happened, as, for instance, *Balan* and *Laban*. The usual form of the first name is Tervaga(u)nt or in English Termagant; Tancred, in French, is sometimes Tangré, which, perhaps unfamiliar in 14th century English, might have been twisted into *Tergan, Tergan[t]*, with some memory of the better-known *Tervagant*.

Mouskes, Fulkes or Foucon d'Anjou married a beautiful demon whom, while hunting, he found by a fountain in a wood¹ (cf. the tale of the first Offa). It is a fact that his daughter Cécile married Tangré d'Andioce,² ancestor of the Tancred whom Richard knew. Here are elements enough for confusion.³

Considering, together with this episode, the names which suggest an origin later than the work of Chretien de Troyes, and perhaps than that of Renauld de Beaujeu,⁴ I judge that the immediate original of *Emaré* arose between 1200 and 1250.

I incline also to think that it was, if a lay, at least much longer than the English, and that the minstrel knew it imperfectly or only in outline. On this point there is but little evidence, one way or the other; but the abruptness with which the account of the robe is thrust into the narrative suggests that something has been omitted for purposes of condensation,⁵ the presence of many curious details and scraps strongly suggestive of French,⁶ taken with the large per cent. of repetitions in which scarcely a word is changed, suggest an attempt to fill out the outline of a larger work, with imperfect knowledge of its details.⁷

§ 8. ORIGINS.

The ramifications of this tale extend so far back and so widely, that the extensive researches of Prof. Suchier, Dr. Gough and

---

[1] *Chronique Rimée* (13th century), ll. 18720–809.
[2] *Op. cit.*; l. 18363.
[3] Curiously enough the name of Arthur is associated with the episode. Benedict says: "Rex autem Angliae dedit ei (*i. e.* Tancred) gladium optimum Arcturi, nobilis quondam regis Britonum, quem Britones vocaverunt Caliburnum" (*loc. cit.*).
[4] Quoted early in the 13th century.
[5] Cf. ll. 78–79 and 187–88. Between ll. 78 and 79, the subject is changed completely, from a description of the Emperor's character, which might lead up very well to l. 188, to an episode not in any way connected with the story as it stands in *Emaré*. Both the lack of connection and the rhymes suggest that at least six lines may have been omitted. Again, there are signs of corruption in ll. 187–88, the metre of the second being spoiled to explain the abrupt change of subject. Since the robe evidently belongs in the narrative, I must suppose that its proper relation has been lost as I suggest above. There are other marks of condensation and alteration, such as in ll. 232–40, the embassy to the Pope and his ready assent without inducement of any sort; ll. 799–804, the exile of the old queen, which is peculiar to this version, and replaces the long account of her punishment which is usually found; ll. 817–22, when the King does penance for a sin that he had not committed. Possibly in the original, as in Enikel's account, he ordered her to be set adrift.
[6] Especially speeches and dramatic details of scenes.
[7] The allusion to an oral source in l. 319 (and possibly in l. 24) if it is not purely conventional, may refer only to the fact that other forms of the tale were being carried about.

others,[1] have by no means exhausted the subject. I can contribute only a little more to the results already obtained and hope to continue the investigation.[2]

To the eighteen[3] mediæval versions analyzed by Suchier, must be added at least two more: *La Filla de l'Emperador Contasti*[4] (Catalan) and a play called *Columpnarium* (Latin).[5]

These twenty pieces, then, may be classified according to their place of origin as follows: Three in England, 12th–15th centuries: *Vita Offae Primi*[6] (*V 1*, 1195–1214, St. Albans, Latin); *Chronique Anglo-Normande*[7] by Nicholas Trivet (*Tr*, 1334–47, French); *Emaré* (*Em*, about 1400, Yorkshire, English).

Four in France, 13th–14th centuries: *La Manekine* by Philippe de Remy, Sire de Beaumanoir[8] (*Man*, about 1270, near Beauvais, French); *La Comtesse d'Anjou* by Jehan Maillart[9] (*Anj*, 1313–16, near Pontoise and Senlis, Normandy, French); *Columpnarium*[10] (*Col*, 14th century, (?) Avignon, (?) Latin); *La Belle Hélène de Constantinople*, (*HC*, 1469, (?) Flanders, French).[11]

Three in Germany, 13th–15th centuries: *Mai und Beaflor*[12] (*Mai*, about 1260, Bavaria or Austria, (?) German); *Die Königstochter von Reussen*, by Jansen Enikel or Enenkel[13] in his *Weltbuch*, or *Universal Chronicle* (*En*, 1277–1300, Vienna, German); *Die Königstochter von Frankreich* by Hans Von Bühel, or "der Büheler"[14] (*Büh*, 1401, Poppelsdorf, near Bonn, German).

---

[1] Suchier, *op. cit.*, p. xxiii ff.; Gough, *Constance Saga*; for kindred folk-tales, Cox, *Cinderella* (*Folk Lore Society*), London, 1893, in addition to the works referred to by Suchier.

[2] In an edition of *La Belle Hélène de Constantinople*.

[3] His No. 19 is a piece of sculpture that might represent *Hung, Ol, Vic, Cont* or even *HC*.

[4] Published by Suchier, *Romania*, xxx, 519–38. Still other versions of the tale are announced to follow.

[5] Mentioned by Creizenach, *Geschichte des Neueren Dramas*, Halle, 1893, I, 533–34 with note. Unpublished. The father is "Emolphus, rex Carillorum;" Phocis and Athens are among the scenes.

[6] Ed. Wats, appendix to *Chronica Majora* of Matthew Paris, London, 1640-39; also *Originals and Analogues* (Chauc. Soc. [1888], pp. 73–84).

[7] *Originals and Analogues*, pp. 2–70.   [8] Ed. Suchier, *op. cit.*

[9] Unpublished. MSS. 765 and Nouv. acquis. 4531, at Paris.

[10] Apparently written for a member of the Colonna family. MS. Lat. 8163. Cf. Creizenach, *loc. cit.*

[11] Unpublished. This is apparently a recension of a much earlier romance, signed "Alexandry manu propria," for "Loyse, Dame de Crequy," who died in 1469 (Lyons MS. 767). It contains much matter relating to the 15th century, and certain episodes seem to refer it definitely to the year mentioned. But I must reserve discussion of this point until I edit the text.

[12] *Dictungen des deutschen Mittelalters*, VII, Leipzig, 1848.

[13] Ed. Von der Hagen, *Gesammtabenteur*, II, 1850, pp. 593–613.

[14] Ed. Merzdorf, Oldenburg, 1867.

EMARÉ.

xxxiv *Origins. English Versions.*

Seven in Italy, 14th–17th centuries: *Ystoria Regis Franchorum et Filie in qua Adulterium Comitere Voluit*[1] (*Yst*, written or copied in 1370, Latin); *Il Pecorone*, Dies X, No. 1, by Giovanni Fiorentino[2] (*Pec*, 1378, Dovadola, Italian); *Novella della Figlia del Re di Dacia*[3] (*Dac*, end of the 14th century, Italian); *Miraculi de la Gloriosa Verzene Maria*,[4] cap. XI (*Mir*, 1475, printed Vicenza, Italian); *De Origine inter Gallos et Britannos Belli Historia* by Bartolomeo Fazio[5] (*Faz*, before 1457, Naples, (?) Latin); *Historia de la Regina Oliva*, by Joannes Florentinus[6] (?) (*Ol*, 16th century, Italian); *La Penta Manomozza* in Basile's *Pentamerone*[7] (*Pen*, before 1637, Naples, Italian).

Three in Spain, 14th–15th centuries: *Historia del Rey de Hungria*[8] (*Hung*, end of the 14th century, Catalan); *Le Victorial* by Gutierre Diaz de Gamez[9] (*Vic*, from before 1435 to 1449, Spanish); *La Filla de l'Emperador Contasti* (*Cont*, 15th century, Catalan).[10]

This shows clearly the progress of the legend. Spreading from England, by the end of the 13th century it had passed through France and Germany, during the 14th century it reached Italy and Spain, died out in Spain in the 15th, but continued in Italy until the 17th; in the 14th also it was revived in England in English,[11] but is not known to have persisted long after 1400.[12]

In tracing out the development of the tale, we find at once

[1] Unpublished. MS. Lat. 8701 at Paris.   [2] Ed. 1378.
[3] Ed. Wesselofsky, Pisa, 1866.   [4] Ed. Vicenza, 1475.
[5] Ed. Camusat, *Bibliotheca Ciaconii*, Paris, 1731. The copy in the British Museum is dated at Amsterdam and Leipzig, 1744, (cols. 893–902).
[6] The poem itself is unpublished, but the play based upon it has been edited by D'Ancona, Pisa, 1863, and included by him in his *Sacre Rappresentazioni*, Florence, 1872, III, 250 ff.   [7] Ed. Liebrecht, Breslau, 1846.
[8] Ed. Bofarull y Mascaró, *Documentos Literarios en Antigua Lengua Catalana*, Barcelona, 1857, pp. 53–59.
[9] Ed. Lemcke, *Bruchstücke aus den noch ungedruckten Theilen des Vitorial von Gutierre Diez de Games*, Marburg, 1865, p. 20; also translated into French by Counts de Circourt and de Puymaigre, Paris, 1867, Livre II, ch. 26, p. 258.
[10] Grouped according to language, 4 are Latin, *VI, Yst, Col, Faz;* 4 are French, *Man, Anj, Tr, HC;* 3 German, *Mai, En, Büh;* 5 Italian, *Pec, Dac, Mir, Ol, Pen;* 2 Catalan, 1 Spanish, *Hung, Cont, Vic:* 1 English, *Em*. Classified according to form, 6 are romances: *Man, Anj, HC, Mai, Büh, Em ;* 6 are attempts to reduce romance material to history: *VI, Yst, Faz, Tr, Vic* (prose), and *En* (verse); 5 are *novelle: Pec, Dac, Pen, Hung, Cont;* 2 are dramas, *Col, Ol;* one is a prose *miracle, Mir*.
[11] Tr's French was quickly translated into English prose by an unknown writer, and into verse by Chaucer and Gower.
[12] These dates refer to the literary versions only, not to the folk-lore, in which it lives on in many countries.

numerous and important differences between *V 1* on the one hand, and *Tr* and *Em* on the other; also between *V 1*, and *Man, Mai* and the original *HC* (**HC*). It is impossible that *V 1* should have developed into these other forms without important influence from outside.

Taking first the English versions, we find the following fundamental differences: (1) the exposure is twice in the forest (*V 1*) instead of twice on the sea (*Tr, Em*); (2) there are two children (*V 1*), one child (*Tr, Em*); (3) they are cut to pieces and brought to life by a miracle, and the heroine is twice threatened with such a death and twice spared (*V 1*); there is no such mutilation (*Tr, Em*); (4) they are protected by a hermit (*V 1*), by a Roman (*Tr, Em*); (5) the scene is entirely localized in England (*V 1*), in part at Rome (*Tr, Em*).

It seems probable that *V 1* was written down largely from oral tradition in English, which may or may not have survived in definite poetical form. The only poem that might be related to it is the eighth century *Wife's Complaint*.[1] This alludes to two definite periods of exile with an interval between, to sorrow for separation from a husband, and to treachery on the part of "kinsmen"; and the heroine seems to be dwelling in a cave in the forest. No names are given, and no children are mentioned; the circumstances of the double exile and the forest chiefly connect this epic fragment with *V 1*.[2] Aside from this, *V 1* is the oldest known form of the legend.

The first problem is to discover, if possible, the origin of the variations enumerated. Certain differences between *Tr* and *Em* can be explained on the basis of a different intermediary, *Em* claiming a "lay" as its original and being certainly derived from the French; *Tr*, "lez Aunciene cronikes de sessounz" or "lestoire de sessouns,"[3] and showing signs of an English original.[4]

---

[1] Cf. *Old English Offa Saga* in *Modern Philology*, June 1904, and January 1905.

[2] But there is no strong evidence against their identity. Cf. *O. E. Offa Saga*, Jan. 1905, p. 45 f. (reprint). *Playn[t] d'Egarye* is "The Exiled Woman's Complaint," cf. p. xx, with note 3, above.

[3] *Originals and Analogues*, p. 3.

[4] This is disputed; but the English sentence on p. 19 seems to favour an immediate source in English not older than the 12th century. This, as Gough suggests (*Constance Saga*, pp. 21–22), may have been a French chronicle of Saxon history; but one slight additional bit of evidence in favour of an English original has been overlooked. *Tr* says that the Saxons called Constance *Couste* (p. 41). But *Couste* is not Saxon. It can scarcely be derived from any other source than the pun in *Li Dis de l'Empereour Coustant:*

xxxvi *Origins. The Constantine Legend.*

An important cycle of legends, which has been recognized to touch that of the Outcast Wife at various points, is that of Constantine the Great (*Const*).[1] Inasmuch as the great majority of the versions agree in general outline with *Tr* and *Em* over against *V 1*, I shall relate briefly the parallel account in *Const* and point out the coincidences in the notes.

Helena, the daughter of a king or nobleman,[2] either goes to Rome on a pilgrimage,[3] or flees thither secretly for some reason,[4] sometimes with a nurse or attendant,[5] and sometimes in disguise.[6] Her child is born under different circumstances, but the parallel is close where the tale describes how she worked with her hands to support and educate the boy, who soon by his gifts attracted the love of all who knew him.[7] With the kidnapping of Constantine, the parallel is lost; but it reappears in the account of the jewels

---

"Et pour çou qu'il ot cousté tant
Li missent il a non Coustant." (ll. 235-36)

If Trivet had found the word *cousté* in its proper context, he knowing French would never have fallen into the blunder that it was Saxon. On the other hand, if his Saxon authority had taken over the word without the pun, he, not associating it with any French source, might easily have assumed that it must be Saxon. This furnishes a bit of evidence for the association of the Constantine legend with the Outcast Wife cycle (cf. *Romania*, VI, 1877, pp. 161–98, on the Constantine legend).

[1] Cf. Suchier, *op. cit.*, p. lxxv, n. 1, and Graf, *Roma nella Memoria e nelle Immaginazioni del Medio Evo*, Torino, 1882-83, II, 46 ff.

[2] For a full account, see Wesselofsky, *Romania*, VI, 101-98; and Coen, *Archivio della Società Romana di Storia Patria*, Roma, 1881, IV, 1-55, 293-316, 535-61; V, 33-66, 489-541.

[3] In *Pec*, the heroine flees in pilgrim's dress; in *Cont*, her explanation of her second exile is "e vaig en pelegrinatge (533)."

[4] "Multi eam clam patriam fugisse affirmant" (Horstmann, *Nova Legenda Anglie*, Oxford, 1901, II, 14).

[5] The nurse is prominent in *HC*, *Mai*, *Anj*, *Yst*, *Dac*, *Em*, *Col*.

[6] So in *Pec*, *Faz*, *Dac*. Once in *Const* she is disguised as a man (cf. Coen, *Archivio*, IV, 33 n.); so in *Yst* and in *Büh* (the beginning of the second flight).

[7] The life of the mother and child in Rome agrees in many respects with *Em*, *Tr*, *Mai*, *Man*, *En*, *Yst*, *Pec*, *Büh*, *Ol*, *Faz*, *Cont*; and is traceable in *HC* and *Dac* (13). In *Pen*, the scene is changed but the circumstances are recognizable, as perhaps they are also, though not so clearly, in *Anj*. *Mir* follows *V 1* in its total disagreement; *Vic* does not contain the second exile, and *Col* I have not seen. Most of these agree in allowing the lapse of many years (from 7 to upwards of 30) between the parting of husband and wife, and contain a description of the youth and education of the boy (*Anj* alone agrees with *V 1* and *Mir* in leaving but a short time).

In *Man*, the heroine is a housekeeper, in *Büh* a servant, in *HC* a washerwoman and a beggar; she also begs in *Büh* and in *Cont*; in *Dac* and *Faz* she is a nurse; in *Em* a nurse and does beautiful embroidery; in *Anj*, she does embroidery and teaches it during the first exile, and in the second depends upon charity. In *Mai*, *En*, *Tr*, *Yst*, *Ol*, she is dependent upon charity; in *Pen* she is the queen's maid during the first exile, and depends upon charity in the second. The attractiveness of the child is everywhere prominent.

brought across the sea by the young princess of Constantinople,[1] and of the exquisite needlework with which she supports the family;[2] in Constantine's attracting the attention of his father, the emperor Constantius on a public occasion;[3] in the reunion of the family at a banquet,[4] and in the recognition by means of a ring.[5] The emperor makes Constantine his heir, and according to some accounts then first marries the mother.[6]

Thus it appears that (1) the substitution of one child for two,[7] (2) the absence of mutilation, hermit and miracle,[8] (3) the life of the woman and child under humble circumstances, and the boy's education at Rome, and the recognition through the son at a banquet by means of a ring, are all accounted for on the hypothesis

[1] Such jewels appear in most of the versions; in *Pec* the woman lives by the sale of jewels inherited from her mother, as in *Const* the princess, by those given by her mother. In several versions, a priceless jewelled robe is especially described (notably *Em, Mai, En, Anj*). In *Const*, the empress of Constantinople gives her daughter "de vasis vestibus et aliis quibuscumque apparatibus auro et argento et gemmis pretiosissimis adornatis ... addens et de thesauris pannorum sericeorum," etc. (*Incerti Auctoris de Constantino Magno ejusque Matre Helena Libellus*, ed. Heydenreich, Lipsiae, 1879, p. 10, ll. 14-21). In another version, the emperor gives Helena instead of a ring a peplum of imperial purple (Coen, *op. cit.*, IV, p. 298).

[2] Here the needlework, prominent in *Anj, Büh, Em, Yst* (perhaps hinted at in *Man*, ll. 5880-84), is transferred to the daughter-in-law, the description of her work, however, being in perfect accord: "Nurus vero Helenae in textura operum muliebrium sumptuosorum et nobilium secundum quod suam decuit condicionem more subtilitatum Graeciae bene erudita bonam pecuniam de labore manuum cottidie lucrabatur" (p. 20, ll. 9-12). Other versions must have attributed it to Helena herself, as there are traditions that she was a famous needlewoman. An embroidered Madonna said to be of her making is still shown at Vercelli, and an inventory of the treasures of Philip the Good contains an altar-cloth attributed to her (cf. Michel, *op. cit.*, II, 336, with note 6).

[3] The recognition comes about through the son, in *Man, Tr, Büh, Em, Ol, Faz, Pen*, and in *HC* (under very different circumstances); and the boy is prominent in *Mai* and *En*.

[4] The banquet is found in *Mai, Man, En, Anj, Tr, Em, Ys, Büh, Faz, Ol, Pen* and in *HC* (the recognition of the sons only).

[5] The ring is a device in *Man, Cont* and *Ol* (in *HC* it is on the arm which Brice carries, and leads to recognition).

[6] In *HC*, this seems to be echoed in the story of the Oriental princess Plaisance. She gives herself to Constantine, but in a moment of peril flees from him across the sea; she lives with a senator in Rome, where her son is born; and after many years of separation, hardship and wanderings, meets Constantine at Rome and marries him. Here is the *senator* who appears in *Man, Tr* (with a wife *Helena*) in *Mai* and in *En* (where the child is *Constantine*). *Iurdan* may even be a corruption of his name (in *HC*) *Joseran*.

[7] *Mai, En, Man, Anj, Tr, Huny, Dac, Büh, Em, Ol, Faz, Cont, Pen* (13) have one; *V 1, HC, Yst, Pec*, and *Mir* (6) have two.

[8] In *Mai, En* (I do not consider scratching the face and cutting the hair an equivalent, as it meant only temporary disfigurement and required no miracle), *Anj, Tr, Büh, Em, Faz, Cont* (though the hand is brought in curiously by the trying on of the mother's glove which exactly fits).

of influence from *Const.*[1] The exposure in an open boat or cask I take to be from an entirely different source,[2] but some of the versions in which the heroine escapes by flight[3] may have come under the influence of *Const.*

Further, the influence of *Const* appears plainly in the names: in *HC*, we have Helena and Constantine, who is also sometimes called Constans, in evident confusion with his father, and Constantinople, of which the heroine's father is emperor; in *Tr*, Tiberie Constantine and Constance[4] (Couste), and Helena[5] her cousin; in *KR* (the prose version dependent upon the source of *En*) the boy is baptized Constantine;[6] in *Cont*, the girl's father is the Emperor Contasti.[7] In *Ol*, the emperor is Giuliano = Julian, who succeeded Constantine, after the short reign of the former's three sons, and married his daughter Helena.[8]

Another possible connection between the two cycles is this. In many of the folk-lore tales, the heroine is an inn-keeper's daughter.

---

[1] *Mai, En, Man, Tr, Yst, Pec, Büh, Em, Ol, Faz, Cont* (11); in *HC* and *Dac*, in part; in *Anj*, the poverty only; in *Hung*, a convent; in *V 1* as in *Mir*, the woods of Britain; in *Pen*, in woods, but afterwards at the house of a sorcerer whose abode is quite unlike that of a hermit. Further, a pagan (witness the case of Vergil) was far more likely to have been transformed into a magician than was a hermit.

[2] See p. xliii below. [3] *HC, Yst, Pec, Dac, Faz.*

[4] Perhaps *Tr*'s confusion arose in part from the duplication of the names in connection with the two emperors: Constantine the Great had a sister Constancia, a daughter Constantina and three sons, Constantius, Constantine and Constans; Tiberius Constantine, a daughter Constantina. The unique opening incident in *Tr* is perhaps to be explained by some legend of the Emperor Maurice and his wife Constantina, who with their children were persecuted and obtained a certain reputation as Christian martyrs. Gough has shown (*Constance Saga*, pp. 34-46) that stories not unlike this in general character were current in the 12th century about Edwin. But he suggests no material that explains the important differences between *V 1* and nearly all the later versions. The only incident for which it might possibly account is the bringing up of the child with a boy of the same age to whom his mother is nurse (in *Dac, Faz*, and in part, in *Mai*). It is possible that more evidence on the Edwin-saga may be forthcoming; but with the facts known at present I cannot accept this as the foundation of the great bulk of the versions. Further, it seems to me that Trivet may have known that he was foisting the tale upon history, for at the end (p. 43) he suddenly introduces Edwin, without accounting for him in any way.

[5] So with Helena. It was the name of Constantine the Great's mother and one of his daughters; of Tiberius Constantine's wife, according to one account, which mentions also a jealous mother-in-law (Gibbon, *op. cit.*, V, 17, with n. 34); likewise, of the wife of Constantine Porphyrogenitus (944), who might have helped on the legend. Is Erayne in *Em* a corruption of Elayne?

[6] Cf. *Mai und Beaflor*, p. xxii.

[7] And merchants take the place of the rudderless boat. This may have come from *Const* or from *Florence of Rome*.

[8] A.D. 355. A contemporary legend is attached to her name to the effect that all her children were killed at birth by the jealousy of her sister-in-law, the Empress Eusebia. See Gibbon (1896-98), II, 258-59, 406-7. This might have helped on the legend of Helena.

Suchier explains this as a natural interpretation in later times of the fact that the letters were changed at the old woman's dwelling, hence she must have been an innkeeper;[1] but in the popular tales it is the heroine, not the traitress, who is connected with the inn. Now Helena is called *stabularia* by St. Ambrose, who was born within twenty-five years of her death;[2] and later writers who wished to argue for her lawful marriage as more consonant with sainthood tried to explain the word away. Hence the association was pretty well established.[3]

That *Const* is as old as the Outcast Wife tale is probable. The legend of the finding of the Cross began in the 4th century,[4] the legend of Constantine's birth was alluded to by Bede[5] early in the 8th century, certain episodes of the cycle were worked up by Cynewulf,[6] a little later, while a Greek legend, apparently of the same century, the martyrdom of St. Eusignius of Antioch, tells a well-defined story not unlike the one I have outlined. In this, Helena is the beautiful daughter of an innkeeper, and Constantius gives her a peplum of royal purple. Years after, wanting an heir to his kingdom, he sends messengers in quest of one. At the inn, their attention is attracted by Constantine, who mounts one of their horses. When they would reprove him, Helena tells his origin, and shows the peplum; and he is adopted by the emperor.[7]

Having proved that *Const* accounts for the differences between *V 1* and *Mir*, and the great majority of versions, we may note that the juxtaposition rather than blending of the two stories is most visible in *HC*, in which we find the two children, the mutilation, hermit and miracle, combined with exposure at sea and sojourn at Rome, together with the episode of the senator, which is transferred to the parallel tale of Plaisance and Constantine. All this matter is connected with legends of St. Martin, possibly by confusion with another empress of the same name.[8]

[1] *Op. cit.*, p. lxvii. [2] Graf, *op. cit.*, II, 53.
[3] Horstmann, *NLA*, II, pp. 13–14.
[4] Cf. Smith and Wace, *Dic. of Christian Biog.*, Constantine the Great.
[5] *Hist. Eccles.*, IV, 523. [6] *Elene*.
[7] Coen, *op. cit.*, IV, 297–98. For other early references and variants, cf. Graf, *op. cit.*, pp. 46–120. Graf shows how from a *stabularia*, Helena came to be considered a princess of Treves or Britain, or the East, her estate growing with the legend.
[8] Sulpicius Severus (*Dialogues*, II, ch. 6, 7) relates how the empress waited upon Martin at table and afterwards dined off the fragments. According to a Welsh tradition (cf. Gibbon, *op. cit.*, III, 136, note) she was called Helena. The passage is suggestive of *HC* in several ways; but more evidence is needed to establish a connection.

Gough supposes that *HC arose at Tours, carried thither from England during the English domination of Touraine, 1154–1205, and this is possible.[1] But I think we may trace the connection further back.

Two of the English versions place some of the scenes in Yorkshire; the third seems to have been written in that very district.[2] *HC certainly arose at Tours. Now the literary connection of York and Tours, in the personality of Alcuin at the end of the eighth century, is one of the important facts of the Dark Ages.[3] It meant that practically the whole of the lore of Northern England at that time was transferred—very literally in the form of copies—to Tours, whence it would readily spread over the Continent.[4]

Const flourished very early in Britain and was particularly connected with York;[5] hence some form of it was almost certain to have been among Alcuin's books. Whether he took also sagas of Offa of Ongle is far more doubtful. He would not have approved of their pagan character;[6] and it is impossible to say how far they had developed by the time of Offa of Mercia. Certainly the legend in *V 1* as we have it, is not alluded to at that time, as is the combat by the river,[7] though the *Wife's Complaint*, which is of the eighth century, shows that similar stories were current then.[8]

In England, before 1200, we have *V 1* quite uninfluenced by *Const*, which, however, appears much later in *Tr* and *Em*. On the continent, Mélusine-tales were early attached to Foulques d'Anjou, and perhaps through his devotion to St. Martin of Tours, his legend came to be bound up with matter relating to that saint, and with *Const*, brought to Tours by Alcuin (as in *HC*). But *Man*, though on a much larger scale, barring certain changes due to the author and the episode of the cut hand (taken perhaps from *HC*),

---

[1] But it does not seem to me to explain the divergences between three versions as closely related in time and place as *HC, Man* and *Anj*.

[2] *V 1, Tr* and *Em*. Historically, the connection with York and the expedition against the Picts and Scots (cf. *Tr, Büh* and doubtless *Pec*) may have been taken from the career of Constantine, but it is curious to note that in Trivet's time (1318) the Scots invaded Yorkshire and burned Knaresborough.

[3] Cf. Gaskoin, *Alcuin*, London, 1904, p. 55.

[4] *Ibid.*, quoting a letter written by Alcuin, p. 100 (Jaffé, *Monumenta Alcuiniana*, Berlin, 1864, p. 346. He urges that his books be sent him from York to Tours that they may be known in France as well as in England.

[5] Gibbon, *op. cit.*, I, 399 ff.

[6] Cf. Gaskoin, pp. 39, 40, 52, 104.

[7] Contained in the first part of *V 1*. In *Widsiþ*, ll. 35–45.

[8] That the legend underlying the *Wife's Complaint* is closely allied, even if not the same, is undeniable.

agrees closely in its general outline with *Em*;[1] also, the source of *Mai* and *En*, although further removed by processes of translation, and modified by other matter, preserves a form between *Em* and *Man*,[2] while *Anj* shows no close essential connection with *Em* or *Tr* and relates itself, if to any form, to *V 1*, which may have been derived from England, direct but late and imperfect, by the Sieur de Viarmes et Chambly.[3]

It is not necessary here to follow out the later developments in great detail.[4]

[1] There are good reasons for holding that Beaumanoir spent several years in England (Suchier, *op. cit.*, I, p. x); and the probable date of his story, 1261–65, would have been shortly after the French lay was composed. But even if he knew the lay, Beaumanoir probably altered and augmented it, partly by fancy, partly according to other traditions.

[2] That is, it preserves some features that have been lost, obscured, or altered in *Man*, particularly *Mai* which retains the robe and the nurse. Cf. Suchier and Gough, *Constance Saga*, for the relationships of *Man*, *Mai* and *En*, which are indisputable. The late *Büh* seems to me purely a combination of forms similar to *Man* (but earlier than Beaumanoir, as the cut hand is lacking) and *Tr*. It would seem natural to suppose that he had used *Mai* and *En*, but the differences are important. It agrees with *Yst* and *Pcc* in identifying the heroine with the daughter of a King of France; but aside from this, in few essentials. If the author was a soldier in the English army (cf. Gough, *Constance Saga*, pp. 28–30) he may have got there a version akin to *Tr*'s original.

[3] Who took part in negotiations with the English in 1303. The romance as it stands is so full of local colour and incidents that might have come from the poet's observation, that it would seem his lord told him only an outline corresponding roughly to *V 1*, in so far as it gives the story of an innocent woman twice exiled in the forest. It retains the primitive feature, in that there is no talk of the Pope or of marriage. The nurse is prominent, though she is dropped abruptly at the time of the marriage (as in *Em*, but later) and the treasure and needlework are emphasized. The account of the teaching of needlework to the seneschal's daughter here resembles the tale of *Berte*, wherein the seneschal's wife is called Constance. Possibly it is *Berte* that borrows this episode, together with a closely associated meeting with a hermit in the forest, from some earlier form of the Outcast Wife tale. In *Anj*, there is no mutilation and but one child, the circumstances and details differ totally from every other version, and the second exile is very short. The unnatural father dies of grief soon after, the traitress is the aunt, the girl flees into the forest the first time, and the second is condemned to be thrown with her child into a well in the forest, the countess is besieged before she is burned (in *Büh*, *Ol*, *Cont* also, but perhaps suggested in each case by *HC*, in which she is first imprisoned in a castle, then burned); the count seeks his wife in the garb of a serf, and the meeting happens in a *Hôtel Dieu*. This poem looks more like a genuine work of creation than any other version; but some of its matter may have been derived from the gestes of the early Dukes of Anjou, which seem to be a mine of tradition as yet largely unexplored.

[4] The changes of scene make a study in themselves. Aside from England, Rome and Constantinople, we find Greece early introduced, doubtless as connected with Constantinople. But *Man* makes the father King of Hungary. This might have come through *Berte*, whose father was King of Hungary, or through *Florence*, in which Emere and Miles belong to that country. It is noteworthy that legend made St. Martin also son of a King of Hungary (cf. especially *Le Mystère de la Vie et Hystoire de Monseigneur Sainct Martin*, 15th century, ed. Boisthibault, Paris, 1841), and that even

xlii   *Origins. Italian and Spanish Versions.*

The Italian and Spanish versions are secondary, derived from the forms already discussed, so blended, condensed, augmented and inverted that their exact relationship is extremely difficult to follow.

In Italy, the oldest account seems to be the greatly condensed *Yst*,[1] which in general reads like a condensation of *HC. Then comes *Pec*[2] also borrowed from *HC. *Dac* is a thoroughly mixed version, but most of its elements are found in *HC*, though differently arranged and combined there.[3] When Fazio came to compile his artificial and arbitrary version, he had certainly *Dac* and *Pec*, possibly several other versions before him.[4] *Ol* gathers up into itself features borrowed from *Mir*, *Florence of Rome*, *Em* and *Cont*.[5] *Mir* stands absolutely apart and belongs to this cycle only

---

St. Helena was, according to some writers, said to have been born in that land (cf. Graf. *op. cit.*, II, 54 ff.). But the idea of the Roman Empire was perhaps the basis for them all (cf. *Huon de Bordeaux*, in which Julius Caesar is King of Hungary and Austria, and "Sire" of Constantinople).

[1] It combines a voyage by land and one across the sea with a mariner. The two sons are educated by a cardinal. Its chief difference is a connection with the Hundred Years' War; but this is sufficiently explained by the date at which it was written. The duke whom the heroine marries might have been conceived as one who also ruled England. Richard Cœur de Lion was called *Comte d'Anjou* (cf. Tarbé, *Chansons de Blondel de Nécle*, Reims, 1862, pp. 129, 151); and the French origin of the girl might have been derived from the Holy Roman Empire (cf. *Mir*, "nel tempo nel quale fo translat(at)o el romano imperio al re de Franzia"). It is not certain that *HC was connected with Constantinople.

[2] The opening incident is altered. The girl flees to avoid marrying an old German lord; otherwise the tale is a fair condensation, with minor changes. One son is called Lionetto (cf. Leo in *HC*).

[3] It shows however a certain influence from the source of *Mai*, in that the heroine, who has but one child, becomes nurse to another about the same age. On what ground Gough derives it from the same source as *Hung* I cannot see. It contains much extraneous religious material.

[4] From *Pec* he seems to have taken the convent episode; and from *Dac* the woman's acting as nurse to a child the age of her own. But he seems to have inverted deliberately the leading parts in order to fit them with his idea of the Hundred Years' War.

[5] From *Mir* it evidently gets the two cut hands and the method of recovery, the exposure in the forest of Britain or Brittany (stanzas of the older *Stella*, the dramatization of *Mir*, are embodied); from *Florence of Rome*, the episode of the scorned knight killing the child of which she is the nurse, and getting her banished to the woods as a result; from *Cont* apparently, the besieging of the mother and burning her in her convent, the use of the ring and perhaps the merchants who took her to the King of Castile. The cask seems to have been borrowed from *En*, unless it comes directly from *Apollonius of Tyre*. The conclusion at Rome again seems to follow *Cont*. Wesselofsky holds that it was also influenced by the legend of Saint Oliva of Palermo. Aside from the name, the chief point of contact is in the double persecution by land and by sea. The saint first crosses the sea (but under different circumstances, "e patria abducta, atque in Africam deportata") and is afterwards driven into a wild forest where she lives as a hermit for years (Fazellus, *De Rebus Siculis*, Catanae, 1749-53, II, 303). It is probable that the slight resemblance warranted the attachment of the name Oliva; but there are no special traces of the legend itself.

in its second part, the first coming from the kindred tale of the cruel stepmother.[1]

Of the Spanish versions, *Vic* in its details suggests *Hung* which depends very directly upon *Man*, though by its own assertion it goes back to a French original, probably *Man*.[2] *Cont* represents a French version older than *Man* and in several respects comes so curiously close to *Em* as to suggest that it depends upon an original nearly related to that of *Em*.[3]

But among all these relationships[4] there is nothing that suggests the difference already observed in the method of exposure. I have alluded to the fact that by the end of the 12th century, the legends of the two Offas had become thoroughly confused.[5] The ancient story of Thrytho from *Beowulf* was transferred to Offa of Mercia, and confused with some legend of a Frankish princess relating to that same King and Charlemagne. I have elsewhere tried to point out the historic and legendary basis of such a tale. As it stands in *V 2*,[6] it shows several curious coincidences with the Outcast Wife series: (1) in *V 2*, the heroine says that she was exiled because of a certain marriage which "ne degeneraret, sprevit." The verbs here suggest the opening incident in the series. It is not likely that Charlemagne would have tried to marry her to a man of low rank.[7] But if the allusion is to pride of race as in *Beowulf*, *En* stands alone in an extraordinary agreement:

"des muotes ward sie alsô reich, (cf. Mōd Đrȳðo wæg).
Daȝ sie kainen man wolt' nemen,
wan der ir ȝe mann(e) möcht' geȝemen."[8]

---

[1] It approaches *V 1* most nearly, with a different opening episode borrowed from some tale similar to *Little Snow-White*. It differs in the important points that (1) the heroine's hands are cut off, but her children are safe; (2) the duke goes to a tournament at the court of his father-in-law, instead of the wars in the North; (3) the duke leaves her in his father's care. *Mir* does not follow *V 1* in representing the war as occurring some time after the birth of the children, or the treachery as coming from the girl's father. It resembles *V 1* chiefly in the hunting episode and the part of the hermit.

[2] The placing the hands on a dish before the King probably comes from *Hung*.

[3] An Anglo-Norman *lai* of the reign of Henry III (whose wife and sister-in-law were both princesses of Provence) might easily have been conveyed to the South of France, thence translated into Catalan.

[4] The detailed comparisons instituted by Suchier, and followed up by Gough with great minuteness, I have not thought it necessary to repeat, as my results agree except where I have called attention to the differences.

[5] Cf. *O.E. Offa Saga*, Jan. 1905, p. 18 ff. (reprint).

[6] That is *Vita Offae Secundi* (of Mercia, 767–96) in Wats's edition.

[7] And he was accused of incest; so likewise was Arthur (aside from *Emaré*).

[8] Ll. 14–16. *Beowulf*, l. 1931 f.; cf. also the prose: "Diu wolte ouch keinen man nemen denne der ir geviele" (pp. ix, x).

Again, in *V 2*, the real reason of her exile is said to be "crimen flagitiosissimum";[1] in *Hung*[2] and *Cont*,[3] she describes herself as a wicked woman and in *En* is described by the queen-mother as "ain boeseȝ weip."[4]

In *V 2*, "addicta est iudicialiter morti ignominiose, uerum ob regie dignitatis reuerentiam igni uel ferro tradenda non iudicatur, sed in nauicula armamentis carente apposit[a],"[5] etc., is very like *Vic*, where the King's Council conclude: "Non es derecho que ansí muera, mas el derecho manda, que muger de linaje real que errare, que la non maten, mas que la metan en una nave sola," etc.[6] So in *Hung*, while some of the barons advise that she be drawn and burned, others, "faes devorar a besties salvatjes," one says put her into a "barcha sens nul govern" and let God take the responsibility.[7] Again, the parents in *V 2* retired to a monastery in their disgust with the marriage;[8] in *Cont*[9] and in *Ol*,[10] the mother retires to a convent.

Even if all these coincidences are accidental, the fact remains that in England in the 8th century and again in the 12th century, we have a legend of a woman charged with a crime, exposed at sea in an open boat,[11] while in the 13th this appears twice (the originals of *Em* and of *Man*), and once in the early 14th (*Tr*), attached to the Outcast Wife Cycle.

The fundamental idea of *V 1* is incest. The whole story is the double vengeance of the baffled father; in *Tr*, it is jealousy (twice repeated) of the mother-in-law;[12] in *Em*, it is first the one then the other.

The source of the incest idea is almost certainly *Apollonius of Tyre*, which was known in England in the 10th or 11th century, and was enormously popular throughout Europe. This is twice at least connected with the tale under consideration: once, in *HC* where

[1] Ed. Wats, p. 12, l. 32 f.
[2] "Fembra pecadriu ere" (ed. Bofarull, p. 60).
[3] In the second journey: "Io son fembre nada de peccat" (*op. cit.*, p. 533). The allusion here, however, may be purely general.
[4] Ll. 271-72. So the prose: "mich hât mîn untât dâ her brâht" (p. xi); and *Mai:* vmb untat ist verstöȝen (col. 68, 7-8).
[5] Ed. Wats, *loc. cit.*   [6] Ed. Lemcke, p. 21.   [7] *Loc. cit.*
[8] Ed. Wats, *loc. cit.*   [9] *Op. cit.*, p. 530.   [10] Ed. D'Ancona, III, 274.
[11] The introduction of the closed boat, which in *En* becomes a cask, may have been suggested by *La Comtesse de Ponthieu* (Moland and D'Héricault, *Nouvelles françoises en prose du xiiie siècle*, Paris, 1856), which in turn may go back to the chest in *Apollonius of Tyre*.
[12] I doubt whether *Tr* is simply repeating his motive. The details of the first part suggest a story akin to the *Kyng of Tars*, possibly related of Maurice and his wife Constance.

the King made his daughter sleep in his room,[1] and in *Yst* where the girl alludes to Antiochus, "pro cum eius filia ipso delicto," etc.[2] Once suggested, the idea related itself in *Em* to similar tales[3] of Arthur, and on the Continent to an Emperor of Rome or King of France, probably through Charlemagne who was both.

The jealous mother-in-law seems to be borrowed from *Mélusine*, or some other early version of the Swan-Maiden Cycle, which flourished in the 12th century.[4] This is seen by the suggestion of monstrous or abnormal children, which is an elementary feature of the tales in which a mortal marries a fay or wood-nymph, the transformed Valkyrie. But the supernatural woman was found sometimes in the forest, sometimes in a ship, as in the legend of Richard Cœur de Lion.[5] Here note that her real name *Bertrade* was perhaps associated with that of the Valkyrie Bertha, as was Cynethryth (= Quendrida in *V 2*) with that of the Valkyrie Thrytho.

The forging of a letter is perhaps a natural device, suggested by the King's absence, and is not necessarily borrowed from *Const* where the use is so different.[6] Still, it is only *V 1* and *Li Dis de l'Empereour Coustant* that it seems to be found as early as the 13th century.

The most difficult problem in the development of the series is the cut-hand episode. In only two of the folk-lore versions, among 43 known to me, is it combined with the incest; on the other hand, it is found regularly where the persecution comes from the step-mother, as in *Mir*, where the hands are used in evidence of death, as in the *Little Snow-White* group; in *Berte*, the heart or tongue (a sow's or dog's used); in the legend of St. Hildegard, the eyes (a dog's used).[7] This with its original significance appears

---

[1] MS. Lyons, 767, fol. 3, 3a, 4a.   [2] MS. Lat., 8701, fol. 142.
[3] The tale of Ragallach (O'Grady, *Silva Gadelica*, London, 1892, 430 ff.) is fundamentally different not only in its details, but in the fact that the king is ignorant of his daughter's identity.
[4] Cf. *O.E. Offa Saga*, pp. 41–43. There is also such a character in *Partonope of Blois*. It is possible, however, that *Const* comes in here as well. The Empress Fausta, wife of Constantine the Great, was believed guilty of the death of her step-son Crispus, and through the agency of Helena, her mother-in-law, is supposed to have been put to death by her husband on a charge of adultery. There was a strong belief shortly after her death that she was innocent, and Chrysostom says that she was exposed in a desert to be devoured by wild beasts (cf. Gibbon, II, 210–11).
[5] See poem of that name (Weber, *English Metrical Romances*, London, 1810, II, ll. 63–229), with Mouskes, *op. cit.*, ll. 18720–809.
[6] Here the order of death to the bearer, is replaced by the command that he of the letter is to marry the princess.
[7] Cf. *O.E. Offa Saga*, p. 44, n. 1.

nowhere in the cycle except in *Mir* and in very clumsy form in *HC*, where, however, it is followed logically by the feature that the cut-hand intended as evidence of execution, with its ring becomes a means of identification. Elsewhere this mutilation occurs only in *Man*, where it is explained by the mediæval idea that no cripple could succeed to a throne;[1] in *Hung*, *Ol*, *Vic* and *Pen* where it is motived by the hypothesis that the beauty of the hands especially attracted the father (brother);[2] hence in these last both hands are cut.

In *V 1*, the idea seems to be fundamentally different. The children are killed by having their hands and feet cut off, and this is the punishment apparently twice threatened for the heroine, but never carried out.[3] This was not done to furnish evidence of death, but merely as a punishment, possibly with the additional idea of preventing escape; incidentally, it opened up the way for a miracle.

The miracle indeed is the link between the two ideas; and the cut-hand was retained long after the original reason for it was forgotten, in order that the miracle might be worked. This hypothesis at least seems to me in accord with the facts; and therefore I hold that the episode as it stands represents two very old Germanic ideas—(1) a definite form of inflicting death, and (2) mutilation as evidence of death, strangely transformed in some cases, but preserved for the miraculous opportunity it furnished.[4]

The other principal legends which influence the series are *Berte* and *Florence of Rome*. *Berte* seems to be the oldest known form of a legend akin to the wicked step-mother tale. Its influence is seen possibly in the mutilation or threat of injury; in *Anj*, perhaps, in the finding of the heroine in the woods by the seneschal and the subsequent episode in which she teaches his daughters embroidery.[5] Perhaps it appears also in the incident of the false charge of murder and the bloody knife (though in *Tr*, this is obviously parallel to *Florence of Rome*),[6] the heroine's concealment of her

[1] Cf. the legend of St. Melor (Brewer, *Dic. of Miracles*, London, 1884, p. 411).
[2] In this respect, it agrees in idea with number LVII of the *Exempla* of Jacques de Vitry (London, 1890).   [3] Wats, *op. cit.*, p. 6, ll. 30-36.
[4] In Brewer's *Dic. of Miracles*, pp. 224, 259, 399, 400, are related various miracles of this sort. The one most likely to have influenced this cycle is perhaps that of St. William of Oulx, in the 12th century, whose hand was miraculously restored (400).
[5] Cf. *O.E. Offa Saga*, p. 44, and p. xli, note 3, above.
[6] The numerous points of contact between these two groups of tales about innocent persecuted women call for detailed discussion, which would be out of place here. *HC*, particularly, is indebted to *Florence of Rome*.

royal birth (not in *V 1*, but common to most of the other versions, and the burning of the traitress (unless this comes from the Swan Cycle). The influence of *Florence* is seen in the heroine's turning nurse (as in *Dac*, *Faz*, *Ol*), and this may share with *Berte*, the *Swan legend*, *Octavian* and *V 1* responsibility for the forest exposure. *Octavian* is responsible for the shipwreck on the island, and for the education of the boys by a hermit in *HC*, possibly also for the substitution of twins for one child.[1]

Without pursuing the subject into further labyrinths,[2] I must touch upon the relation between the English poems nearly contemporary with *Em*, *Sir Eglamour of Artas* (*Eglam*) and *Torrent of Portyngale* (*Tor*), which contain the episode of the princess with her child (children) exposed at sea.

With the important difference that in *Eglam* and *Tor* the woman is guilty of the fault for which she is exposed, there are so many coincidences of detail and language as to suggest borrowing: whole lines and couplets agree, with only such slight changes as come often between two versions of one story.[3] In *Eglam* and *Tor*, the passage is episodic, as one among the many difficulties encountered by the knight in winning his lady; hence I hold that the source of *Em* is perhaps the original of the three. *Eglam* shows much closer resemblances than *Tor*, which agrees however in dialect, *Eglam* being classed as Northern. Pending a critical edition of the latter, I will add only that the resemblances between

[1] In *V 1* the children are not said to be twins.
[2] Other legends appear in *HC*: *St. Alexius*, *Eustache-Placidas*, possibly *La Reine Sibille*, possibly *Richard Cœur de Lion*, and others that I have not yet identified.
[3] Cf. *Em*, 1. 634; *Eglam*, 1. 827; *Tor*, ll. 1838–39; *Em*, ll. 326, 674; *Eglam*, l. 887; *Em*, ll. 277–78; *Eglam*, ll. 881–82; *Tor*, ll. 1840–41; *Em*, ll. 317, 322; *Eglam*, l. 884; *Tor*, l. 1843; *Em*, l. 275; *Eglam*, l. 883 (emend *then odur*, copied by mistake from l. 884 to *ne rodur*); *Em*, l. 314; *Eglam*, l. 885; *Em*, ll. 328, 676; *Eglam*, l. 888; *Em*, ll. 355, 364, 718; *Eglam*, l. 887; *Em*, ll. 331, 337; *Eglam*, l. 897; *Em*, ll. 368–70; *Eglam*, ll. 928-29 (the word *delycyus* is not common in romances of this class). I might add a long list of lines in *Eglam* which are paralleled in *Em* but are less peculiar or significant. Cf., however, *Eglam*, l. 801; *Em*, l. 33; *Eglam*, l. 803; *Em*, l. 624; *Eglam*, l. 815; *Em*, l. 639; *Eglam*, l. 818; *Em*, 646; *Eglam*, ll. 844–45; *Em*, ll. 772–74; *Eglam*, ll. 938–39; *Em*, ll. 343–45, 688–90, etc. There are also longer passages that read like an echo from *Em* or its sources: the King of Egypt's discovery of the outcast, l. 892 f.; the child serving in the hall at dinner, ll. 1273–75; and especially, the mother's instructions to her son how he should greet his father, ll. 1278–81. That these episodes are borrowed rather from the French than from the English *Em* is perhaps indicated by the use made of the ring (*Eglam*, 715–17, *Tor* 1396–98) which is not found in *Em*, but appears in several other versions (see p. xxxvii, note 5, above).

Eglam and *Tor* not found in *Em*, and the greater remoteness of *Tor* from *Em*, indicate that, whatever may be the relations of the two in other respects, *Eglam* was probably the intermediary for *Tor* in this episode.

§ 9. CONCLUSION.

Emaré cannot be ranked high among the versions of this tale. Over against *La Comtesse d'Anjou*, it is rough indeed, although in contrast with the artificial elaborations of *La Belle Hélène* and even of *La Manekine*, its simplicity, even baldness, is refreshing; and in a few instances it shows real tenderness.[1] But it is interesting chiefly from the point of view of origins. I am convinced that further work upon the development of the legend, would throw light not only upon the close relations between the great cycles of romance, but also upon the methods used in the combination of the ancient national lore with the "boke of Rome" (the importance of which has been recognized only within the last 25 years),[2] and to some extent with Oriental tales brought westward in the Crusades, and with early or contemporary history;[3] and would show how these classes of materials were modified, even transformed, under the influence of the Church, its dogmas and legends.[4]

[1] Notably in the references to the child. Cf. ll. 661-2 and 811-13.

[2] The researches of Coen and Graf particularly indicate that the phrase meant more than a casual reference to a French source. From numerous hints and allusions in mediæval literature, I am convinced that some great collection of Roman tales, of which the extant *Gesta Romanorum* is but a feeble imitation or reflection, has been lost; and that this contained matter relating to various historical personages, especially Julius Caesar, Octavianus, Vespasian, Hadrian, Titus, Diocletian, Nero and Constantine (in the *Comte de Poitiers*, Constantine frees his uncle Nero from the prison of the Sultan of Babylon, Graf, *op. cit.*, pp. 52-71, and see note on l. 158), and perhaps Julian and others. But as yet the classical element in romance has not received the attention bestowed upon the Celtic and Teutonic materials.

[3] A most amusing combination of materials is mentioned by Graf (*op. cit.* II, 47): Constantine's sword was given by Hugh Capet to Athelstan, and used by Guy of Warwick to kill Colbrand.

[4] I believe that the Provençal legend of the two Maries (mothers of St. James the Greater and St. James the Less), which tells how they were driven from Palestine by the Jews, put out to sea in an open boat without sail or rudder or provision, and under divine guidance drifted to the village now called *Les-Saintes-Maries-sur-Mer*, has exerted some appreciable influence, at least, upon the popularity of the cycle; but at present my facts are too disconnected to be presented in an orderly manner here. The Provençal legend seems to be connected with some worship of *Notre Dame de la Mer*. An interesting suggestion of this is offered by a bas-relief, taken from a 16th century house in Lyons (now in the museum of that city). It shows the Madonna and Child alone in a little ship, which is being governed by two angels. The inquiry is perhaps worth pursuing.

APPENDIX.

THE play contained in MS. Latin 8163 of the Bibliothèque Nationale, formerly of the Colbert collection, and officially catalogued as apparently of the 15th century, is preceded by the notice in a later hand :

"Columnarium quod et comoedia sine nomine inscribitur, sex actibus absolvitur, non inelegante scriptis, stilo tamen nonnihil impedito. Codex scriptus xiiii saeculo."

The *Prologue*, which explains the moral purpose of the play, is headed by a picture of a monk who seems to be dictating to a cardinal writing at a desk. The Colonna coat-of-arms (a white column on a red ground) occurs frequently throughout the 49 folios of the work. As the text is written without any spacing between the parts, the length of the piece is apparent.

Passing through Paris, I was able to give a few hours to a cursory examination of this version ; but the *Argument*, immediately following the *Prologue*, seems to show that it probably contributes little to our knowledge of the development of the legend. It can therefore be passed over with a few brief comments, more especially as it will doubtless be included by Professor Suchier among his studies on *La Fille sans Mains*, of which another is announced to appear shortly in *Romania*.

The plot in outline is as follows : " Emolphus, rex Carillorum," at the entreaty of his dying wife Phylostates, swears that he will marry only a woman like herself ; and so presently, after a search throughout the world, chooses his own daughter Ermionides. She and her nurse pretend to agree, on condition that he finds it to be the will of the gods ; and while he is gone to consult the oracle, they escape in a boat to Phocis. Here they are kindly received by Sophia ; and Ermionides is married to Hor(r)estes (Orestes), king of that country, to the great anger of his mother Holicomesta or Olicomesta (almost certainly corrupted from Clytemnestra). A son is born while Hor(r)estes is absent in Athens ; and the mother-in-law forges a letter to say that the child is an Ethiopian, and then changes the king's order to take care of mother and child, into a command that they be put to death. Accordingly Celius ("regine custos") sets the boy adrift in an osier-basket, with gold and regal treasures, and abandons the queen in a trackless wood. The child is found by Acthironeus (?), who takes him to Parnassus to consult the oracle upon the question of his adoption. Meanwhile, Hor(r)estes, upon his return, is informed by Celius of what has occurred, and wishes to avenge himself by the death of his mother, but oppressed by the Furies ("stipatus manipulor*um* cohorte ferocium"), he is soothed by the counsel of Celius, and persuaded to go to the oracle at Parnassus. Here he finds his wife and son ; and the nurse presently coming with news of the death of Emolphus, and "Phocays senex," with word of the death of Olicomesta, the play ends happily for hero and heroine.

There are many characters in the play, and some of the names have a curious interest, as: Pallinurus (the boatman), Misenus, Cornelius Tacitus, Tertullus, Verginus, Afrodissa (Aphrodite?), Regulus, etc. Especially noteworthy is the name Altruda, which seems to be a Germanic form related to the Drida of *Vita Offae Secundi*. Perhaps when the text is printed, more light on this point may be forthcoming.

The chief peculiarities of this version are: (1) the apparently unique combination of the tale of the persecuted wife with that of Orestes and Clytemnestra, and (2) the attempt to reconcile conflicting accounts of the method of exposure in the case of mother and child, unless, indeed, in the case of the latter, the author borrows the device from the narrative of Moses.

Altogether, this text belongs to the group in which there is only one child and no cut-hand; but it does not agree, in setting or in details, with any other work that has been published. For this reason, it may possibly prove to be of more value than I have assigned to it on the basis of the *Argument* alone.

Emare.

(MS. Cotton Caligula, A ii.)

(1)

Ihesu, þat ys kyng in trone,
As þou shoope boþe sonne *and* mone,
   And alle þat shalle dele *and* dyghte,   3
Now lene vs grace such dedus to done,
In þy blys þat we may wone,
   Men calle hyt heuen lyghte;   6
And þy modur Mary, heuyn qwene,
Bere our arunde so bytwene,
   That semely ys of syght,   9
To þy sone þat ys so fre,
In heuen wyth hym þat we may be,
   That lord ys most of myght.   12

[leaf 71]
Jesus, who created all things,
grant us grace to enter heaven.
Mother Mary, intercede for us with thy Son.

(2)

Menstrelles þat walken fer *and* wyde,
Her *and* þer in euery a syde,
   In mony a dyuerse londe,   15
Sholde, at her bygynnyng,
Speke of þat ryghtwes[1] kyng
   That made both see *and* sonde.   18
Who-so wylle a stounde dwelle,
Of mykylle myrght y may ȝou telle,
   And mornyng þer a-monge;   21
Of a lady fayr *and* fre,
Her name was called Emare,
   As I here synge in songe.   24

Minstrels who wander in many lands, should
first invoke the Creator.
Whosoever will stop a while shall hear a tale of mirth and sorrow, about a fair lady called Emaré.

[1] R. ryhtwcs.

(3)

Her father was an emperor called Sir Artyus, who had great possessions.	Her fadyr was an emperour, Of castelle *and* of ryche towre, 　　Syr Artyus was hys nome; He hadde boþe hallys *and* bowrys, Frythes fayr, forestes wy*th* flowrys, 　　So gret a lord was none.	27 30
He had married a fair and courteous lady, Dame Erayne.	Weddedde he had a lady, That was boþ fayr *and* semely, 　　Whyte as whales bone; Dame Erayne hette þ*at* emper*es*, She was fulle of loue *and* goodnesse, 　　So curtays lady was none.	 33 36

(4)

Sir Artyus was the best man in the world, brave	Syr Artyus was þe best ma*n*ne In þe worlde þat lyuede þa*n*ne, 　　Both hardy and þer-to wygȟt;	 39
and courteous and just.	He was curtays in alle þyng, Bothe to olde *and* to ȝynge, 　　And welle kowth dele *and* dygȟt.	 42
He had but one child of his wedded wife; but that was fair and seemly,	He hadde but on chyld in h*y*s lyue, Be-geten on h*y*s weddedde wyfe, 　　And þat was fayr and brygȟt; For soþe, as y may telle þe,	 45
and called Emaré.	They called þat chyld Emare, 　　That semely was of sygȟt.	 48

(5)

When she was born, she was the fairest creature in the land.	When she was of her mod*ur* born, She was þe fayrest creature borne, 　　That yn þe lond was þoo;	 51
The empress died before the child could speak or walk,	The emper*es*, þat fayr ladye, Fro her lord gan she dye, 　　Or hyt kowþe speke or goo.	 54
so it was sent to a lady called Abro,	The chyld, þat was fayr *and* gent, To a lady was hyt sente, 　　That men kalled[1] Abro;	 57

[1] R. called.

She thaw3tħ hyt curtesye *and* thewe,
Golde *and* sylke for to sewe,
 Amonge maydenes moo.   60

who taught it courtesy and stitchery, among other maidens.

(6)

Abro taw3te þys mayden smalle,
Nortur[1] þ*at* men vseden[2] in sale,
 Whyle she was in her bowre.   63
She was curt*a*ys in all*e* thynge,
Bothe to olde[3] *and* to 3ynge,
 And whythe as lylye flowre;   66
Of her hondes she was slye,
All*e* he[r] loued þ*a*t her sye,
 Wyth menske *and* mychyl honou*r*.   69
At þe mayden leue we,
And at þe lady fayr *and* fre,
 And speke we of þe emp*er*our.   72

Abro gave this small maiden the usual education.

She was courteous to everybody,

white as a lily, clever with her hands, and loved by all.

Now let us leave the maiden and her nurse and speak of the emperor,

(7)

The emp*er*our of gentyll*e* blode,
Was a curteys lorde *and* a gode,
 In all*e* maner of thynge.   75
Aftur, when hys wyf was dede,
And ledde hys lyf yn weddewede,
 And[4] myche loued playnge,—   78
Sone aft*ur*, yn a whyle,
The ryche kynge of Cesyle
 To þe emperour gan wende.   81
A ryche present w*yth* hym he browght,
A cloth þat was wordylye wroght.
 He wellecomed hym as þe hende.   84

who, after his wife's death, led his life in widowhood, and greatly loved dalliance.

Soon after, the great king of Sicily came to the emperor,

[leaf 71, bk.] bringing a splendid cloth as present, and was nobly welcomed.

(8)

Syr Tergaunte þat nobyll*e* kny3t (hy3te),[5]
He presented þe emp*er*our ryg*h*t,
 And sette hym on hys kne,   87

Sir Tergaunte, that noble knight, on his knee before the emperor,

---

[1] R. Nortour.   [2] R. usedenn.   [3] R. old.
[4] G. *changes* And *to* He. *Other possible emendations are* : And he ledde; *or, by analogy to l.* 989, A ledde.
[5] *The omission of* hy3te *improves the metre; but although the* y3 *is blotted, the word is not unmistakably crossed out by the scribe. Kölbing, however, considers it erased* (*Eng. Stud.*, xv, 248). *See note on the line.*

4 *The King of Sicily's splendid Cloth given to Emaré's Father.*

<small>offered the splendid cloth, which was as thickly set as possible with topaz and rubies,</small>
Wyth þat cloth rychyly dyght,
Fulle of stones þer hyt was pyght,[1]
    As thykke as hyt myght be: 90
Of(f)[2] topaze and rubyes,

<small>with toad-stones and agate (?) and other rich stones,</small>
And oþur stones of myche prys,
    That semely wer to se;   93
Of crapowtes *and* nakette,
As[3] thykke ar þey sette,

<small>as I tell thee truly.</small>
    For sothe, as y say þe.   96

(9)

<small>As the emperor looked at the cloth, he could not see readily for the glistering of the rich stones,</small>
The cloth was dysplayed sone,
The empe*rour*[4] lokede þer-vpone,
    And myght[e] hyt not se;   99
For glysteryng of þe ryche ston
Redy syghte had he non),

<small>and said, "How may this be?"</small>
    And sayde, "How may þys be?"   102
The empe*rour* sayde on hygh,

<small>Certes, this is a fairy thing or an illusion."</small>
"Sertes, þys ys a fayry,
    Or ellys a vanyte!"   105

<small>The King of Sicily answered, "It is the richest jewel in christendom."</small>
The Kyng of Cysyle answered þan,
"So ryche a jwelle ys þer non
    In alle Crystyante."   108

(10)

<small>The daughter of the Emir of heathendom made this cloth, and adorned it with gold, azure and precious stones,</small>
The amerayle dow3ter of heþe*n*nes
Made þ*y*s cloth w*yth*-outen) lees,
    And wrow3te hy*t* alle w*yth* pride;   111
And p*ur*treyed hyt w*yth* gret honour,
Wyth ryche golde and asowr,

<small>which were sought far and wide.</small>
    And stones on ylke a syde.   114
And, as þe story telles in honde,
The stones þat yn þys cloth stonde,
    Sow3te þey wer fulle wyde.   117

<small>Seven years it was a-making, before it was finished.</small>
Seuen wy*n*ter hy*t* was yn makynge,
Or hy*t* was browghte to endynge,
    In herte ys not to hyde.   120

---

[1] MS., was dye (*crossed out*) pyght.   [2] G. Of.
[3] G. *suggests* A[l]s[ō] *for* As *to improve the metre. See ll.* 90, 138.
[4] R. emperoer.

(11)

In þat on korner made was	In the first corner were the true lovers, Ydoyne and Amadas, portrayed with true-love-flower in precious stones,
Ydoyne and Amadas,	
Wyth loue þat was so trewe; 123	
For þey loueden⟩ hem wyth[1] honour,	
Purtrayed[2] þey wer wyth trewe-loue-flour,	
Of stones bryȝht of hewe : 126	
Wyth carbunkulle and safere,	carbuncle, sapphire, chalcedony and clear onyx, set in new gold, diamonds, rubies, and other precious stones.
Kassydonys and onyx so clere,	
Sette in golde newe; 129	
Deamondes and rubyes,	
And oþur stones of mychylle pryse,	
And menstrellys wyth her gle[we]. 132	

(12)

In þat oþur corner was dyȝht,	In the second corner were the true lovers; Trystram and Isowde, set thickly with precious stones,
Trystram and Isowde so bryȝt,	
That semely wer to se; 135	
And for þey loued hem ryȝht,	
As fulle of stones ar þey dyȝht,	
As thykke as þey may be : 138	
Of topase and of rubyes,	with topaz, rubies, and other gems,
And oþur stones of myche pryse,	
That semely wer to se ; 141	
Wyth crapawtes and nakette,	with toadstones and agate (?).
Thykke of stones ar þey sette,	
For sothe, as y say þe. 144	

(13)

In þe thrydde korner, wyth gret honour,	In the third corner were Florys and Dame Blawnchefour, with true-love-flower in gems, "knights and senators," potent emeralds,
Was Florys and Dam Blawncheflour,	
As loue was hem be-twene; 147	
For þey loued[3] wyth honour,	
Purtrayed þey wer' wyth trewe-loue-flour,[4]	
Wyth stones bryȝht and shene : 150	
Ther wer' knyȝtus and senatowres,	
Emerawdes of gret vertues,	
To wyte wyth-outen⟩ wene ; 153	

[1] R. wit.   [2] G. Pourtrayed.
[3] G. supplies hem after loued by analogy to l. 124 above.
[4] R. flower.

diamonds, coral, chryso- lite, crystal, and good garnets.

Deamoundes[1] and koralle,
Perydotes and crystalle,
  And gode garnettes by-twene.   156

(14)

In the fourth corner was the son of the Sultan of Babylon, and the Emir's daughter, who made this cloth for his sake.

In the fowrthe korner was oon,
Of Babylone þe sowdan sonne,
  The amerayles dowȝtyr hym by.   159
For hys sake þe cloth was wrowght;
She loued hym in hert and thowght,
  As testymoyeth þys storye.   162

[leaf 72]
An unicorn, with his high horn, was portrayed before the maiden, with flowers and birds in rare stones.

The fayr mayden her by-forn
Was portrayed an vnykorn,
  Wyth hys horn so hye;   165
Flowres and bryddes on ylke a syde,
Wyth stones þat wer sowghte wyde,
  Stuffed wyth ymagerye.   168

(15)

When the cloth was finished, it was brought to the sultan's son. "My father took it by force from the sultan, and gave it me, and I bring it to thee specially."

When the cloth to ende was wrowght,
To þe sowdan sone hyt was browȝt,
  That semely was of syȝte.   171
"My fadyr was a nobylle man,
Of þe sowdan he hyt wan,
  Wyth maystrye and wyth[2] myȝth.   174
For gret loue he ȝaf hyt me,
I brynge hyt þe in specyalte,
  Thys cloth ys rychely dyght."   177

He gave it to the emperor, who thanked him properly.

He ȝaf hyt þe emperour,
He receyued hyt wyth gret honour,
  And þonkede hym fayr and ryȝt.   180

(16)

The King of Sicily amused himself with the emperor as long as he wished,

The Kyng of Cesyle dwelled þer,
As long as hys wylle wer,
  Wyth þe emperour for to play;   183
And when he wolde wende,

then took leave and went home.

He toke hys leue at þe hende,
  And wente forth on hys way.   186

---

[1] R. Deamondes.   [2] R. omits.

Now remeueth¹ þys nobylle kyng.
The emperour aftur hys dowȝtur hadde longyng,²
    To speke wyth þat may.   189
Messengeres forth he sent
Aftyr þe mayde fayr³ and gent,
    That was bryȝt as someres day.   192

Now the emperor longed to speak with his daughter, and sent messengers to fetch her.

(17)
Messengeres dyȝte hem in hye ;
Wyth myche myrthe and melodye,
    Forth gon þey fare,   195
Both by stretes and by stye,
Aftur þat fayr lady,
    Was godely vnþur gare.   198
Her norysse, þat hyȝte Abro,
Wyth her she goth forth also,
    And wer sette in a chare.   201
To þe emperour gan þe[y] go ;
He come aȝeyn hem a myle or two ;
    A fayr metyng was there.   204

These went forth, with mirth and minstrelsy, to fetch the fair lady. Abro, her nurse, went with her, and they set out in a "car," to go to the emperor, who came a mile or two to meet them.

(18)
The mayden, whyte as lylye flour,
Lyȝte aȝeyn⁴ (her fadyr⁵) þe emperour ;
    Two knyȝtes gan her lede.   207
Her fadyr, þat was of gret renowne,
That of golde wered þe crowne,
    Lyȝte of hys stede.   210
When⁶ þey wer bothe on her fete,
He klypped her and kyssed her swete,
    And bothe on fote þey ȝede.   213
They wer glad and made good chere,
To þe palys þey ȝede in fere,
    In romans as we rede.   216

The maiden, white as a lily, alighted, and was led up by two knights. Her father also alighted, and when they were both on foot, "clipped" her and kissed her, and they went together to the palace.

(19)
Then þe lordes þat wer grete,
They wesh and seteñ don⁷ to mete,
    And folk hem serued swyde.   219

The great lords washed and sat down to meat.

---

¹ *So MS., not* remeneth *as G. says.*
² *This line is obviously corrupt.* G. *omits* aftur hys dowtȝur and inserts *he after* emperour.   ³ R. fayre.   ⁴ G. aȝeyen.
⁵ G. *suggests the omission of these words.*
⁶ G. Then.   ⁷ R. doun.

8 *Emaré's Father gets the Pope's Leave to wed her. She refuses.*

<small>The maiden sat before her father,</small>
The mayden, þat was of sembelant[1] swete,
Byfore[2] her owene fadur sete,
<small>and she was so fair that he fell in love with her,</small>
    The fayrest wommon on lyfe;   222
That alle hys hert *and* alle hys þowȝth,
Her to loue was yn browght;
    He by-helde her ofte syþe.   225
So he was an-amored hys þowȝtur tylle,
<small>and wished to make her his wife.</small>
Wyth her he þowȝth to worche hys wylle,
    And wedde her to hys wyfe.   228

(20)

<small>When the meal was done,</small>
And when þe metewhyle was doñ,[3]
In-to hys chambur he wente soñ,[4]
<small>he called his council into his chamber, and bade them get leave from the Pope for him to wed his daughter.</small>
    And called hys counseyle nere.   231
He bad þey shulde sone go *and* come,
And gete leue of þe Pope of Rome,
    To wedde þat mayden clere.   234
Messengeres forth þey wente,
<small>They durst not disobey, but sent messengers, and earls with them, to Rome. They brought the Pope's Bull permitting the marriage.</small>
They durste[5] not breke hys commandement,
    And erles wyth hem yn fere.   237
They wente to þe courte of Rome,
And browȝte þe Popus Bullus sone,
    To wedde hys dowȝter dere.   240

(21)

<small>Then the emperor was glad, and had a robe made of the cloth of gold,</small>
Þen was þe emperour gladde *and* blyþe,
And lette shape a robe swyþe,
    Of þat cloth of golde;   243
And when hyt was don her vpon,
<small>in which she looked fairer than mortal woman.</small>
She semed non erþely wommon,
    That marked was of molde.   246
<small>Then he said, "Daughter, I will wed thee;"</small>
Then seyde þe emperour so fre,
" Dowȝtyr, y wolle wedde þe,
    Thow art so fresh to be-holde."   249
<small>[leaf 72, bk.]</small>
Then sayde þat wordy vnþur wede,
<small>and she, "Nay, God forbid!</small>
" Nay, syr, God of heuen hyt for-bede,
    Þat euer do so we shulde!   252

---

    [1] G. semblant.   [2] G. Before.   [3] R. doun.
    [4] R. soun.   [5] R. durst.

(22)

Ȝyf hyt so be-tydde þat ȝe me wedde, *If we should marry, we should both be lost.*
And we shulde play to-gedur in bedde,
   Bothe we were for-lorne!   255
Þe worde shulde sprynge fer *and* wyde, *The news would go all over the world.*
In alle þe worlde on euery syde,
   Þe worde shulde be borne.   258
Ȝe ben a lorde of gret pryce, *You are a great lord; let not such sorrow arise.*
Lorde, lette neuur such[1] sorow a-ryce,
   Take God ȝou be-forne!   261
That my fadur shulde wedde me, *God forbid that my father should marry me!*
God forbede þat I hyt so se,
   That wered þe crowne of þhorne[2]!"   264

(23)

The emperour was ryght wrothe, *The emperor was furious, and swore great oaths that she should die. He had a boat made, and put her therein, in her splendid dress, without food or drink; and cast her into the sea without anchor or oar.*
And swore many a grete othe,
   That deed shulde she be.   267
He lette make a nobulle boot,
And dede her þer-yn, God wote,
   In þe robe of nobulle ble.   270
She moste haue wyth her no spendyng,
Noþur mete ne drynke[3];
   But shate[4] her yn-to þe se.   273
Now þe lady dwelled þore,
Wyth-owte anker or[5] ore,
   And þat was gret pyte!   276

(24)

Ther come a wynd, y vnþurstonde, *A wind arose and blew the boat out of their sight.*
And blewe þe boot fro þe londe,
   Of her þey lost þe syght.   279
The emperour hym be-þowght *The emperor bethought himself, and grieved so at his misdeed that he fell to the earth in a swoon.*
That he hadde alle myswrowht,
   And was a sory knyȝte.   282

---

[1] R. suche.   [2] R. thorne.
[3] MS. drynke. R. *adds* [givyng]. G. *suggests* n[ōþ]e[r]. Cf. *l.* 593 *below. I should suggest* dryukyng *in the sense of something to drink; but the first instance of this use quoted in the Oxford Dictionary is* 1552. *See note on the line.*   [4] R. shote.
[5] G. *suggests* ō[þe]r ōre, *which improves the metre.*

                    And as he stode yn studyynge,
                    He felle down in sowenynge,
                        To þe yrþe was he dyght.   285

The great lords that stood by, took him up and comforted him.
                    Grete lordes stode þer-by,
                    And toke v[p]¹ þe emperour hastyly,
                        And conforted hym fayr and ryght.   288

(25)

When he was recovered, he wept sore and said, "Alas, my daughter! Alas, that I was made man!
                    When he of sownyng kouered was,
                    Sore he wepte and sayde, "Alas,
                        For my dowhter dere!   291
                    Alas, þat y was made man!
                    Wrecched kaytyf þat I hyt am!"
                        The teres ronne by hys lere.   294

I went against God's law, and she was true. Alas, that she were here!"
                    "I wrowght² a-ȝeyn Goddes lay,
                    To her þat was so trewe of fay.
                        Alas, why ner³ she here!"   297
                    The teres lasshed out of hys yȝen;

The great lords wept with him.
                    The grete lordes þat hyt syȝen,
                        Wepte and made ylle chere.   300

(26)

There was none that did not weep for that comely maid.
                    Ther was noþur olde ny ȝynge,
                    That kowþe stynte of wepynge,
                        For þat comely vnþur kelle.   303

They thronged into ships to seek her; but although they sought everywhere on the sea, they came back without her.
                    In-to shypys faste gañ þey þrynge,
                    For to seke þat mayden ȝynge,
                        þat was so fayr of flesh and felle.   306
                    They her sowȝt ouur-alle yn þe see,
                    And myȝte not fynde þat lady fre,
                        A-ȝeyn þey come fulle snelle.   309

Now let us leave the emperor and speak of the lady.
                    At þe emperour now⁴ leue we,
                    And of þe lady yn þe see,
                        I shalle be-gynne to telle.   312

(27)

She floated forth alone, praying to God and His mother.
                    The lady fleted forth a-lone;
                    To God of heuen she made her mone,
                        And to hys modyr also.   315

---

¹ MS. vn.   ² R. wrawght.   ³ MS. vowel blotted.
⁴ MS. *inserts in the margin, with a caret to show that it should be placed between* emperour *and* leue.

She was dryuen wyth wynde and rayn,
Wyth stronge stormes her a-gayn,
    Of þe watur so blo.   318
As y haue herd menstrelles syng yn sawe,
Hows ny lond myȝth she non knowe,[1]
    A-ferd she was to go.   321
She was so dryuen fro wawe to wawe,
She hyd her hede and lay fulle lowe,[2]
    For watyr she was fulle woo.   324

(28)

Now þys lady dwelled þore,
A good seuen-nyȝth and more,
    As hyt was Goddys wylle;   327
Wyth carefulle herte and sykyng sore,
Such sorow was here ȝarked ȝore,
    And euer lay she stylle.   330
She was dryuen yn-to a lond,[3]
Thorow þe grace of Goddes sond,
    That alle þyng may fulfylle;   333
She was on þe see so harde be-stadde,
For hungur and thurste almost madde,
    Woo worth wederus ylle!   336

(29)

She was dryuen in-to a lond,
That hyȝth Galys, y vnþurstond,
    That was a fayr countre.[4]   339
Þe kyngus steward dwelled þer by-syde,
In a kastelle of mykylle pryde;
    Syr Kadore hyght he.   342
Euery day wolde he go,
And take wyth hym a sqwyer or two,
    And play hym by þe see.   345
On a tyme he toke þe eyr,
Wyth two knyȝtus gode and fayr;
    The wedur was lythe of le.   348

---

[1] R. knawe.   [2] R. lawe.
[3] L. 331, in MS. is followed by l. 338 crossed out.
[4] R. cuntre.

(30)

and found a boat ashore, in it a glistering thing that amazed them; but they went up to the lady, who had been so long "meatless," that it grieved them to see she was almost dead.	A boot he fond by þe brym,
	 And a glysteryng þyng þer-yn,
	     Ther-of þey hadde[1] ferly. 351
	 They went forth on þe sond
	 To þe boot, y vnþurstond,
	     And fond þer-yn þat lady. 354
	 She hadde so longe meteles be,
	 That hym þowht gret dele to se;
	     She was yn poyn[t] to dye. 357

They asked her name; but she changed it to Egaré.	They askede her what was her name; She chaunged hyt þer a-none, And sayde she hette Egare. 360

(31)

Sir Kadore, full of pity, took the lady home.	Syr Kadore hadde gret pyte; He toke vp þe lady of þe see, And hom gan he[r] lede. 363
She was lean as a tree through lack of food.	She hadde so longe meteles be, She was wax lene as a tre, That wordy vnþur wede. 366

They took her into a room of the castle, and fed her with all kinds of delicious meat and drink.	In-to hys castelle when she came,
	 In-to a chawmbyr þey her nām,
	     And fayr þey gan[2] her' fede, 369
	 Wyth alle delycyus mete *and* drynke,
	 That þey myȝth hem on þynke,
	     That was yn alle þat stede. 372

(32)

When the fair lady was recovered,	When þat lady, fayr of face, Wyth mete *and* drynke keuered was, And had colour a-gayne, 375

she taught them to sew and mark all kinds of silk-work. They were full fain of her; she was courteous to all,	She tawȝte hem to sewe *and* marke
	 Alle maner of sylky[3] werke;
	     Of her þey wer fulle fayne. 378
	 She was curteys yn alle þyng,
	 Bothe to olde *and* to ȝynge,
	     I say ȝow for certeyne. 381

[1] R. had.   [2] R. gann.
[3] R. sylkyn. MS. sylky, *but a letter has evidently been erased after it.*

She kowȝþe¹ werke alle maner þyng,
That felle to emperour, or to kyng,
    Erle, barown) or swayne.   384

and could do work suited to emperor, king, earl, baron, or swain.

(33)

Syr Kadore lette make a feste,
That was fayr *and* honeste,
    Wyth hys lorde, þe kynge.   387
Ther was myche menstralse,
Tro*m*mpus, tabo*urs*² *and* sawtre,
    Bothe harpe *and* fydylleyng.   390
The lady, þat was gentyll*e and* smalle,
In kurtulle alone serued yn halle,
    By-fore þat nobulle kyng.   393
Þe cloth vpon) her shone so bryȝth,
When she was þ*er*-yn y-dyȝth,
    She semed non erdly þyng.   396

Sir Kadore made a goodly feast for the king, with minstrelsy of trumpet, tabour, psaltery, harp, and fiddle. The gentle lady, in her kirtle alone, served before the king; but in her shining robe she seemed no earthly thing.

(34)

The kyng loked her vp-on),
So fayr a lady he syȝ neu*ur* non),
    H*y*s herte she hadde yn wolde.   399
He was so an-amered of þat syȝth,
Of þe mete non he myȝth,
    But faste gan her be-holde.   402
She was so fayr and gent,
The kynges loue on her was lent,
    In tale as hyt ys tolde.   405
And when þe metewhyle was don),³
In-to þe chamb*ur* he wente son),⁴
    And called h*y*s barouns bolde.   408

The king looked at her, and became so enamoured of her fairness that he could not eat, but stared at her fixedly. When the meal was done, he went into the chamber and called his barons,

(35)

Fyrst he calle[d] Syr Kadore,
And oþ*ur* knyȝtes þat þer wore,
    Hastely come hym tylle.⁵   411
Dukes *and* erles, wyse of lore,
Hastely come þe kyng be-fore,
    And askede what was h*y*s wylle.   414

Sir Kadore, and other knights to come hastily to him; and wise dukes and earls came and asked the king's will.

---

¹ R. kowthe.   ² R. Trompus, tabors.
³ R. doun.   ⁴ R. soun.
⁵ MS., *l.* 411 *is omitted and written in the margin.*

Then he said to Sir Kadore, "Tell me whence is that lovely maid [leaf 73, bk.] that served in hall to-day?"	Then spakke þe ryche yn ray, To Syr Kadore gan he say, Wordes fayr *and* stylle : " Syr, whēns ys þat louely may, That yn þe halle serued þys day ? Telle me, ȝyf hyt be þy wylle."	417 420

(36)

Then said Sir Kadore : "An earl's daughter from a far land. I sent for her to teach my children courtesy. She is the cunningest woman in her work that I have seen in christendom." Then said the king : " I will make her my queen."	Then sayde Syr Kadore, y vnþurstonde, " Hyt ys an erles þowȝt*ur* of ferre londe, That semely ys to sene. I sente aft*ur* her, certeynlye, To teche my chylderen curtesye, In chambur wyth hem to bene. She ys þe konnyngest wommon, I trowe, þat be yn Crystendom, Of werk þat y haue sene." Then sayde þat ryche raye, " I wylle haue þat fayr may, And wedde her to my quene!"	423 426 429 432

(37)

The king sent for his mother,	The nobulle kyng, verament, Aftyr[1] hys modyr he sent, To wyte what she wolde say.	435
and showed her the fair maid in her shining robe.	They browȝt[e] forth hastely That fayr mayde Egarye ; She was bryȝth as somercs day. The cloth on her shon so bryght, When she was þer-yn dyght, And her-self a gentelle may,	438 441
The old queen said, " I never saw a woman half so fair."	The olde qwene sayde a-now, " I sawe neuer wommon Haluendelle so gay ! "	444

(38)

The old queen said ungraciously, "Son, this is a fiend.	The olde qwene[2] spakke word*us* vnhende, And sayde, " Sone, þys ys a fende,[3] In þys wordy wede !	447

[1] R. After.   [2] R. old quene.
[3] MS. *as in text, not* sende *as* G. *says.*

As þou louest my blessynge,	Do not marry her, if you love my blessing."
Make þou neuur þys weddynge,	
Cryst hyt de forbede!" 450	
Then spakke þe ryche ray,	Then the king said, "Mother, I will," and led her forth.
"Modyr, y wylle haue þys may!"	
And forth gan her lede. 453	
The olde qwene,[1] for certayne,	The old queen went home in anger, and would not be present.
Turnede wyth ire hom a-gayne,	
And wolde not be at þat dede. 456	

(39)

The kyng wedded þat lady bryght;	The king married the lady with great purveyance.
Grete puruyance þer was dy3th,	
In þat semely sale. 459	
Grete lordes wer serued a-ryght,	Great lords were well served, and there was a huge crowd,
Duke, erle, baron and kny3th,	
Both of grete and smale. 462	
Myche folke for soþe þer was,	
And þer-to an huge prese,	
As hyt ys tolde yn tale. 465	
Ther was alle maner þyng,	and all thing that belong to a king's wedding, including minstrels.
That felle to a kyngus weddyng,	
And mony a ryche menstralle. 468	

(40)

When þe mangery was done,	After the feast was done, the great lords departed,
Grete lordes departed sone,	
That semely were to se.[2] 471	
The kynge be-lafte wyth þe qwene,	and left the king and queen together in love and joy.
Moch loue was hem be-twene,	
And also game and gle. 474	
She was curteys and swete,	
Such a lady herde y neuur of 3ete;	
They loued both wyth herte fre. 477	
The lady þat was both meke and mylde,	The lady, that was courteous and sweet, conceived a child, as it was God's will.
Conceyued and wente wyth chylde,	
As God wolde hyt sholde be. 480	

[1] R. quene.   [2] R. see.

(41)

The king of France, at that time beset with Saracens,	The kyng of France, yn þat tyme, Was be-sette wyth many a Sarezyne, And cumbered alle in tene;	483
sent for the king of "Galys" and other lords.	And sente aftur þe kyng of Galys, And oþur lordys of myche prys, That semely were to sene.	486
The king of "Galys" gathered men from all sides,	The kyng of Galys, in þat tyde, Gedered men on euery syde, In armour bryght and shene.	489
and said to Sir Kadore and other lords, "Take heed to my queen."	Then sayde þe kyng to Syr Kadore, And oþur lordes þat ther wore, "Take good hede to my qwene."	492

(42)

The king of France sent for them all, king, knight, and clerk;	The kyng of Fraunce spared none, But sent for hem euerychone, Both kyng, knyȝth and clerke.	495
but the steward remained at home to take care of the queen.	The stward[1] by-laft at home, To kepe þe qwene whyte as fome, He come not at þat werke.	498
She went with child, according to God's will,	She wente wyth chylde yn place, As longe as Goddus wylle was. That semely vnþur serke;	501
till she gave birth to a goodly child with a double king's mark.	Thylle þer was of her body, A fayr chyld borne and a godele, Hadde a dowbylle kyngus marke.	504

(43)

They christened him Segramour with great honour.	They hyt crystened wyth grete honour, And called hym Segramour; Frely was þat fode.	507
[leaf 74] Then Sir Kadore made in haste a noble letter and sent it to the king.	Then þe steward, Syr Kadore, A nobulle lettur made he thore, And wrowȝte hyt alle wyth gode. He wrowȝte hyt yn hyȝynge, And sente hyt to hys lorde þe kynge, That gentylle was of blode.	510 513

[1] R. stiward.

Emaré's Mother-in-law forges a Letter about Emaré's Boy. 17

The messenger forth gan wende,
And wyth þe kyngus modur gan lende,
 And yn-to þe castelle he ʒode.   516

The messenger went forth, and stopped at the castle of the king's mother.

(44)

He was resseyued rychely,
And she hym askede hastyly,
 How þe qwene hadde spedde.   519
"Madame, þer ys of her y-borne
A fayr man-chylde, y telle ʒou be-forne,
 And she lyth in her bedde."   522
She ʒaf hym for þat tydynge
A robe and fowrty shylynge,
 And rychely hym cladde.   525
She made hym dronken of ale and wyne,
And when she sawe þat hyt was tyme,
 Tho chambur she wolde[1] hym lede.   528

She received him graciously, and asked how the queen had sped. "Madam, she has a fair man-child, and lies ill." She gave him a robe and forty shillings for that news, made him drunk with ale and wine, and led him to his room.

(45)

And when (s)he was on slepe browʒt,
The qwene þat was of wykked þowʒt,
 Tho chambur gan she wende.   531
Hys letter she toke hym fro,
In a fyre she brente hyt do;
 Of werkes she was vnhende.   534
Anoþur lettur she made wyth euylle,
And sayde þe qwene had born a deuylle,
 Durste no mon come her hende.   537
Thre heddes hadde he there,[2]
A lyon, a dragon and a beere,
 A fowlle, feltred fende.   540

When he was asleep the wicked queen went to his room, and took and burned the letter. Another she made, saying that the queen had borne a devil with three heads (of a lion, a dragon and a bear), and none dared approach her.

(46)

On þe morn, when hyt was day,
The messenger wente on hys way,
 Bothe by stye and strete;   543

On the morrow, the messenger continued his journey

---

[1] R. wole. G. *suggests* she hym led[d]e, *which is better for rhyme as well as for metre.*
[2] MS., *hole in* there, *but the vowel is probably* e.

EMARE.   C

till he came to the king, greeted him, and gave him the letter.	In trwe story as y say, Tylle he come þer as þe kynge laye, And speke wordus swete.	546
As the king read, he wept, and then fell in a swoon because of his sorrow.	He toke þe kyng þe lettur yn honde, And he hyt redde, y vnþurstonde, The teres downe gan he lete. And as he stode yn redyng, Downe he felle yn sowenyng, For sorow hys herte gan blede.	549 552

(47)

Great lords took him up;	Grete lordes þat stode hym by, Toke vp þe kyng hastely; In herte he was fulle woo.	555
but he greeted sore, and said, "Alas, that I was ever born, and made king,	Sore he grette and sayde, "Alas, That y euur man born was! That hyt euur shullde be so!¹	558
and afterwards wedded the fairest thing on earth— that Jesus should send such a foul fiend to come between us!"	Alas, þat y was made a kynge, And sygh wedded þe fayrest þyng, That on erþe myght go! That euur Jhesu hym-self wolde sende Such a fowle, loþly fende, To come by-twene vs too!"	561 564

(48)

When he saw that it might be no better, he made and sealed another letter, commanding	When he sawe hyt my3t no bettur be, Anoþur lettur þen made he, And seled hyt wyth hys sele. He commanded yn alle þynge,	567
that the lady be cared for untill she was well, with folk to wait upon her.	To kepe welle þat lady 3ynge, Tylle she hadde her hele; Bothe gode men and ylle, To serue her at her' wylle, Bothe yn wo and wele.	570 573
The messenger took the letter, and rode home through the same land, by the king's mother's castle.	He toke þys lettur of hys honde, And rode þorow þe same londe, By þe kyngus modur castelle.	576

¹ MS. That hyt euur so shullde be.

(49)

And þen he dwelled þer alle ny3t;
He was resseyued *and* rychely dy3t,
  And wyste of no treson.
He made hy*m* welle at ese *and* fyne,[1]
Bothe of brede, ale *and* wyne,
  And þat be-rafte hy*m* hys reson.
When he was on slepe brow3t,
The false qwene hys lett*ur* sow3t;[2]
  In-to þe fyre she kaste hyt downe.
A-noþ*ur* lett*ur* she lette make,
That men sholde þe lady take,
  And lede her owt of towne.

(50)

And putte her yn-to þe see,
In þat robe of ryche ble,
  The lytylle chylde her' wyth;
And lette her' haue no spendyng,
For no mete ny for drynke,[3]
  But lede her' out of þat kygh.[4]
"Vpon payn of chylde *and* wyfe,
And also vpon 3o*ur* owene lyfe,
  Lette her' haue no grygħt!"
The messenger knewe no gyle,
But rode hom mony a myle,
  By forest *and* by frygħt.

(51)

And when þe messenger' come home,
The steward toke þe lett*ur* sone,
  And by-gan to rede.
Sore he sygħt and sayde, "Alas,
Sĕrtes, þys ys a fowle case,
  And a de[l]fulle dede!"
And as he stode yn redyng,
He felle downe yn swonynge,[5]
  For sorow hys hert gan blede.

---

[1] *Probably* a-fyne, *as* G. *suggests.* Cf. *l.* 913 *below.*
[2] *After* t *in* MS., *a small round blot, which does not seem to be intended for an* e. G., *however,* sow3te.
[3] R. drynkyng.   [4] R. kyght.   [5] R. swounynge.

and they all wept with him for that good woman.	Ther was noþur olde ny ʒynge, That myʒte for-bere of wepynge, For þat worþy vnþur wede.	612

(52)

The lady, hearing the outcry, called to the steward, "What is this?	The lady herde gret dele yn halle, On þe steward gan she calle, And sayde, "What may þys be? ʒyf any-þyng be a-mys.	615
Tell me what is wrong."	Telle me what þat hyt ys, And lette not for me."	618
The steward said, "Here is a letter from my lord that grieves me."	Then sayde þe steward, verament, "Lo, her, a lettur my lord hath sente, And þer-fore woo ys me!"	621
She read how she must into the sea.	She toke þe lettur and by-gan to rede; Then fonde she wryten alle þe dede, How she moste yn-to þe see.	624

(53)

The queen bade him be still,	"Be stylle, syr," sayde þe qwene, "Lette syche mornynge[1] bene; For me haue þou no kare.	627
and do the command of his lord,	Loke þou be not shente, But do my lordes commāundement,[2] God for-bede þou spare!	630
who was ashamed of his "simple lady,"	For he weddede so porely, On me, a sympulle lady, He ys a-shamed sore.	633
and yet would never again get one so gentle of blood.	Grete welle my lord fro me, So gentylle of blo(l)de[3] yn Cristyante, Gete he neuur more!"	636

(54)

There was great weeping and wringing of hands when the lady with her child entered the ship.	Then was þer sorow and myche woo, When þe lady to shype shulde go; They wepte and wronge her hond[e].[4] The lady, þat was meke and mylde, In her arme she bar her chylde, And toke leue of þe londe.	639 642

---

[1] MS., o in mornynge *blotted*.
[2] R. commaundement.   [3] R. blode.
[4] R. honde. MS hondus.

When she wente yn-to þe see,
In þat robe of ryche ble,
   Men sowened on þe sonde. 645
Sore þey wepte *and* sayde, "Alas,
Certys, þ*ys* ys a wykked kase!
   Wo worth dedes wronge!" 648

(55)
The lady *and* þe lytylle chylde
Fleted forth on þe wat*ur* wylde,
   W*yth* ful*le* harde happes. 651
Her surkote þat was large *and* wyde,
Ther-w*yth* her vysage she gan hyde,
   W*yth* þe hynþ*ur* lappes; 654
She was aferde of þe see,
And layde her gruf vpoñ a tre,
   The chylde to her pappes. 657
The wawes, þat were grete *and* stro*n*g,
On þe bote faste þey þonge,[1]
   W*yth* mony vnsemely rappes. 660

(56)
And when þe chyld gan to wepe,
W*yth* sory herte she songe h*yt* a-slepe,
   And putte þe pappe yn h*ys* mowtħ, 663
And sayde, "My3th y on*us* gete lond,
Of þe wat*ur* þat ys so stro*n*ge,
   By northe or by sowthe, 666
Wele owth y to warye þe, see,
I haue myche shame yn the!"
   And eu*ur* she lay *and* growht.[2] 669
Then she made her prayer,
To Ihes*u and* hys mod*ur* dere,
   In al*le* þat she kowþe. 672

(57)
Now þ*ys* lady dwelled thore,
A ful*le* seuene[3] nygħt *and* more,
   As h*yt* was Goddys wylle; 675

---

[1] R. thronge.
[2] G. *emends to* on grōwf, *a reading suggested by Holthausen. See note on this line.*
[3] MS., *a letter seems to have been erased before* nyght.

	Wyth karefulle herte *and* sykyng sore,	
	Such sorow was her' ʒarked ʒore,	
	And she lay fulle stylle.	678
[leaf 75]	She was dryuen toward Rome,	
By God's grace she was driven towards Rome,	Thorow þe grace of¹ God yn trone,	
	That alle þyng may fulfylle.	681
	On þe see she was so harde be-stadde,	
almost mad with hunger and thirst.	For hu*n*gur *and* thurste alle-most madde,	
	Wo worth chawnses ylle!	684

(58)

In that city dwelled a rich merchant called Jurdan,	A marchaunte dw[el]led² yn þat cyte,	
	A ryche mon of golde *and* fee,	
	Iurdan was hys name.	687
who every day went to take the air by the sea.	E(e)uery day wolde he	
	Go to playe hym by þe see,	
	The eyer for to tane.	690
On this occasion,	He wente forth yn þat tyde,	
	Walkynge by þe see syþe,	
he went forth alone,	Alle hym-selfe a-lone.	693
and found a boat with a woe-begone fair lady.	A bote he fonde by þe bry*m*me,	
	And a fayr lady ther-ynne,	
	That was ryght wo-by-gone.	696

(59)

He was frightened	The cloth on her shon so bryth,	
	He was a-ferde of þat syght,	
by the glitter of the bright cloth, and thought she was no earthly being.	For glysteryng of þat wede;	699
	And yn hys herte he þowʒth ryght,	
	That she was non erdyly wyght,	
	He sawe neuu*r* non s(h)uch yn leede.	702
He asked her name, and she said "Egarye."	He sayde, "What hette ʒe, fayr ladye?"	
	"Lord," she sayde, "y hette Egarye,	
	That lye her³ yn drede."	705
Then he took home the fair lady and her child.	Vp he toke þat fayre ladye,	
	And þe ʒonge chylde her by,	
	And hom he gan hem lede.	708

---

¹ MS., o *in* of *is corrected from* y.
² *A hole in MS. where* el *should be.* ³ R. here.

(60)

When he come to hys byggynge,
He welcomed fayr þat lady ȝynge,
    That was fayr and bryght;   711
And badde hys wyf yn alle þynge,
Mete and drynke for to brynge,
    To þe lady ryght.   714
"What þat she wylle craue,
And her mowth wylle hyt haue,
    Loke hyt be redy dyght.   717
She hath so longe meteles be,
That me þynketh grette pyte;
    Conforte her ȝyf þou myght."   720

(61)

Now þe lady dwelles ther,
Wyth alle mete þat gode were;
    She hedde at her wylle.   723
She was curteys yn alle þyng,
Bothe to olde and to ȝynge;
    Her loued bothe gode and ylle.   726
The chylde by-gan for to þryfe,
He wax þe fayrest chyld onlyfe,
    Whyte as flour on hylle;   729
And she s[h]ewed¹ sylke werk yn bour,
And tawȝte her sone nortowre;
    But euyr she mornede stylle.   732

(62)

When þe chylde was seuen ȝer olde,
He was bothe wyse and bolde,
    And wele made of flesh and bone;   735
He was worþy vnþur wede,
And ryght welle kowþe prike a stede,
    So curtays a chylde was none.   738
Alle men louede Segramowre,
Bothe yn halle and yn bowre,
    Wher-so-euur he gan gone.   741

¹ MS. has dots under h, seemingly to show erasure.

24 *The King of Galys is shown his Mother's forged Letter.*

<small>Now let us leave the lady and speak of the king of Galys, when he came home.</small>

Leue we at þe lady, clere of vyce,
And speke of the kyng of Galys,
    Fro þe sege when he come home.   744

(63)

<small>The siege is broken, and the king comes home in triumph,</small>

Now þe sege broken ys,
The kyng come home to Galys,
    Wyth mykylle myrthe and pride.   747

<small>with great lords riding by his side.</small>

Dukes and erles of ryche asyce,
Barones and knyȝtes of mykylle pryse,
    Come rydynge be hys syde.   750

<small>Sir Kadore rode to meet him,</small>

Syr K[a]dore[1], hys steward þanne,
A-ȝeyn hym rode wyth mony a man,
    As faste as he myght ryde ;   753

<small>and told him the news.</small>

He tolde þe kyng a-ventowres,
Of hys halles and hys bowres,
    And of hys londys wyde.   756

(64)

<small>The king blamed him for not speaking first of Egaré,</small>

The kyng sayde, " By Goddys name,
Syr Kadore, þou art to blame,
    For þy fyrst tellynge !   759
Thow sholdest fyrst haue tolde me
Of my lady Egare,

<small>whom he loved best.</small>

    I loue most of alle þyng ! "   762

<small>Then the steward was grieved, and cried: "Are ye no true king ? [leaf 75, bk.] Here is your letter. I have obeyed you."</small>

Then was þe stewardes herte wo,
And sayde, " Lorde, why sayst þou so ?
    Art not þou a trewe kynge ?   765
Lo her, þe lettur ȝe sente me,
Ȝowr owene self þe soþe may se ;
    I haue don ȝour byddynge."   768

(65)

<small>The king read the letter, and turned pale, crying, " Alas, that ever I was born !</small>

The kyng toke þe lettur to rede,
And when he sawe þat ylke dede,
    He wax alle pale and wanne.   771
Sore he grette and sayde, " Alas,
That euur born y was,
    Or euur was made manne !   774

---

[1] MS. Kodore.

Syr Kadore, so mot y the,
Thys lettur come neuur fro me,
 I telle¹ þe her a-none!"   777   This letter never came from me."
Bothe þey wepte and ȝaf hem ylle.
" Alas," he sayde, "saf Goddys wylle!"   They lamented together,
And both þe[y] sowened þen.   780   and then swooned.

(66)

Grete lordes stode by,   The great lords took up the king;
And toke vp þe kyng hastyly,
 Of hem was gret pyte;   783
And when þey both keuered were,   and when the two were recovered,
The kyng toke hym þe letter þer,   the king took
 Of þe heddys þre.   786   the letter
" A, lord," he sayde, " be Goddus grace,   and said that he could not understand it.
I sawe neuur þys lettur yn place!
 Alas! how may þys be?"   789
Aftur þe messenger' þer þey sente,   They sent for the messenger and asked how he went.
The kyng askede what way he went:²
 " Lor,³ be ȝour modur fre."   792   "Lord, by your mother's castle."

(67)

" Alas!" þen sayde þe kynge,   "Alas," said the king,
" Wheþur my modur wer' so vnhende,   "was it my mother then?
 To make þys treson?"   795
By my krowne, she shalle be brent,   She shall be burned without trial!"
Wyth-owten any oþur jugement,
 That thenketh me best reson!" 798
Grete lordes toke hem be-twene,   Great lords decided to exile the queen and attaint her.
That þey wolde exyle þe qwene,
 And be-refe her' hyr renowne. 801
Thus þey exiled þe false qwene,   Thus they did, and deprived her of her property.
And by-rafte her' hyr lyfloþe clene,
 Castelle,⁴ towre and towne.   804

(68)

When she was fled ouur þe see fome,   When she had fled over-sea, the king remained at home, sorrowing
The nobulle kyng dwelled at hom,
 Wyth fulle heuy chere;   807

---

¹ R. tell. ² R. wente. ³ R. Lord.
⁴ MS., between Castelle and towre are the words town & with a dotted line beneath them to signify erasure.

	Wyth karefulle hert and drury mone,	
	Sykynges made he many on,	
for Egaré.	For Egarye þe clere.	810
And when he saw children play, he wept for his son.	And when he sawe chylderen play, He wepte and sayde, "Welle-a-wey,	
	For my sone so dere!"	813
Thus he lived	Such lyf¹ he lyued mony a day,	
	That no mon hym stynte may,	
for seven years,	Fully seuen yere.	816

(69)

till he remembered how his lady was drowned for his sake,	Tylle a thowght yn hys herte come, How hys lady, whyte as fome, Was drowned for hys sake.	819
and he decided to go to Rome for penance.	"Thorow þe grace of God yn trone, I wolle to þe pope of Rome, My penans for to take!"	822
He prepared many ships and filled them with goods for his men,	He lette ordeyne shypus fele, And fylled hem fulle of wordes wele, Hys men mery wyth to² make.	825
gave alms for his soul's sake,	Dolys he lette dyȝth and dele, For to wynnen hym sowles hele,	
and went aboard.	To þe shyp he toke þe gate.	828

(70)

The sailors made ready,	Shypmen,³ þat wer' so mykylle of price, Dyght her' takulle on ryche a-cyse, That was fayr and fre.	831
drew up sail and laid out oar, with a fair wind and fine weather.	They drowȝ vp sayl and leyd out ore, The wynde stode as her' lust wore, The weþur was lyþe on le.	834
They sailed over the salt foam, by God's grace.	They sayled ouer' þe salt fome, Thorow þe grace of God in trone, That most ys of powste.	837
He took his inn at the house of the burgess with whom Emaré dwelled.	To þat⁴ cyte when þe[y] come, At þe burgeys hous hys yn he nome,⁵ Ther-as woned Emarye.⁶	840

---

¹ MS., after lyf a hole, covering space enough for a letter, perhaps e.   ² MS. after to, be crossed out.
³ MS., h is written over y, in Shypmen.   ⁴ R. the.
⁵ L. 837 follows in MS., but is crossed out and underlined.
⁶ G. Emarē.

(71)

Emare called he[r] sone,
Hastely to here come,
    Wyth-oute ony lettynge,   843
And sayde, "My dere sone so fre,
Do a lytulle aftur me,
    And þou sha[l]t[1] haue my blessynge.   846
To-morowe þou shalle serue yn halle,
In a kurtylle of ryche palle,
    By-fore þys nobulle kyng;   849
Loke, sone, so curtays[2] þou be,
That no mon fynde chalange to þe,
    In no manere þynge!   852

(72)

When þe kyng ys serued of spycerye,
Knele þou downe hastylye,
    And take hys hond yn þyn;   855
And when þou hast so done,
Take þe kuppe of golde sone,
    And serue hym of þe wyne.   858
And what þat he speketh to þe,
Cum a-non and telle me,
    On Goddus blessyng and myne!"   861
The chylde wente yn-to þe halle,
Among[3] þe lordes grete and smalle,
    That lufsumme[4] wer' vnþur lyne.   864

(73)

Then þe lordes þat wer' grete,
Wysh and wente to her' mete,
    Men[s]trelles browȝt yn þe kowrs.   867
The chylde hem serued so curteysly,
Alle hym loued þat hym sy,
    And spake hym gret honowres.   870
Then sayde alle þat loked hym vpon,
So curteys a chyld sawe þey neuur non,
    In halle ny yn bowres.   873

---

[1] R. shalt.   [2] R. curteys.
[3] R. Amonge.   [4] R. lufsume.

The king asked his name, and he said, "Segramowres."	he kynge sayde to hym yn game, ' Swete sone, what ys þy name ?" " Lorde,"[1] (he seyd) " y hyȝth Segramowres."	876

(74)

Then the king sighed,	Then þat nobulle kyng Toke vp a grete sykynge,	
for this was his son's name.	For hys sone hyghte so ; Certys, wyth-owten lesynge,	879
He wept and was sorrowful ;	The teres out of hys yen gan wryng ; In herte he was fulle woo.	882
but still he "let be," as he looked at the child and loved him.	Neuer'-þe-lese, he lette be, And loked on þe chylde so fre, And mykelle he louede hym þoo.	885
But he asked the burgess, "Is this thy son?" and was answered, "Yes."	The kyng sayde to þe burgeys a-non, " Swete syr, ys þys þy sone ?" The burgeys sayde, "ȝoo."	888

(75)

Then the great lords washed after meat before the spicery.	Then þe lordes þat wer' grete, W(h)esshen a-ȝeyn aftyr mete, And þen come spycerye.	891
The child kneeled,	The chyld þat was of chere swete, On hys kne downe he sete,	
and served the king so well that he called the burgess, and said : "Give me that little boy, and I will make him a great lord."	And serued hym curteyslye. The kynge called þe burgeys hym tylle, And sayde, " Syr, yf hyt be þy wylle, ȝyf me þys lytylle[2] body ! I shalle hym make lorde of town and towre, Of hye halles and of bowre, I loue hym specyally."	894 897 900

(76)

When he had served the king, he went and told his mother what had happened. "When he shall go to chamber, take his hand, for he is thy father,	When he had serued þe kyng at wylle, Fayr he wente hys modyr tylle, And tellys her how hyt ys. " Soone when he shalle to chambur wende, Take hys hond at þe grete ende, For he ys þy fadur, y-wysse ;	903 906

[1] R. Lord.
[2] MS., *after* lytylle, chylde *is written and crossed out.*

And byd hy*m* come speke wy*th* Emare,
That changed her' name to Egare,
  In the londe¹ of Galys!"
The chylde wente a-ȝeyn to halle,
A-monge þe grete lordes alle,
  And serued on ryche a-syse.

909
912

and bid him come speak with Emaré, who called herself Egaré in Galys." Then the child returned to his serving.

(77)

Whe*n* þey wer' welle at ese, a-fyne,
Bothe of brede, ale *and* wyne,
  They rose vp, more *and* myn.
When þe kyng shulde to chamb*ur* wende,
He toke h*y*s hond at þe grete ende,
  And fayre he helpe hym yn;
And sayde, "Syr, yf ȝo*ur* wylle be,
Take me ȝo*ur* honde *and* go wy*th* me,
  For y am of ȝowr kynne!
Ȝe shulle come speke wy*th* Emare,
That chau*n*ged² her' nome to Egare,
  That berys þe whyte chy*n*ne!"

915
918
921
924

When they were satisfied, they rose up; and when the king was going to his chamber, the child led him in, and gave him Emaré's message.

(78)

The kyng yn herte was full*e* woo,
Whe*n* he herd mynge þo,
  Of her þat was h*y*s qwene;
And sayde, "Sone, why sayst þou so?
Wher'-to vmbraydest þou me of my wo?
  That may neuer' bene!"
Neuur þeles wy*th* hym he wente;
A-ȝeyn hem come þe lady gent,
  In þe robe bryght *and* shene.
He toke her' yn h*y*s armes two,
For joye þey sowened, both to,
  Such loue was hem by-twene.

927
930
933
936

The king was sorrowful when he heard of her who had been his queen; but although he said this was impossible, he went with the child, and the lady came to meet him in her bright robe. He took her in his arms, and they both swooned for joy and love.

(79)

A joyfull metyng was þer þore,
Of þat lady, goodly vnþ*ur* gore,
  Frely in armes to folde.

939

There was great

¹ R. lond.   ² R. changed.

30 *Emaré's Father decides to pray the Pope to forgive him.*

<small>rejoicing over</small> Lorde! gladde was Syr Kadore,
And oþur lordes þat þer' wore,
Semely to be-holde, 942
<small>the recovery of the lady that had been put into the sea.</small> Of þe lady þat wa[s]¹ put yn þe see,
Thorow grace of God in Triuite,
þat was keuered of cares colde. 945
<small>[leaf 76, bk.] Now speak we of the emperor,</small> Leue we at þe lady whyte as flour,
And speke we of (her' fadur) þe emperour,
That fyrste þys tale of y-tolde. 948

(80)

<small>who was now old,</small> The emperour her fadyr þen
Wa[s]² woxen an olde man,
And þowȝt on hys synne; 951
<small>and remembered his sin against his daughter.</small> Of hys þowȝtyr Emare,
That was putte yn-to þe see,
That was so bryght of skynne. 954
<small>He decided to go to the Pope for penance,</small> He þowȝt[e] that he wolde go,
For hys penance to þe Pope þo,
And heuen for to wynne. 957
<small>and sent messengers to find him an inn at Rome.</small> Messengeres he sente forth sone,
And þey come to þe kowrt of Rome,
To take her lordes inne. 960

(81)

<small>Emaré prayed her</small> Emare prayde her lord,³ þe kyng,
"Syr, a-byde þat lordys komyng,
That ys so fayr and fre. 963
And, swete syr, yn alle þyng,
A-qweynte ȝou wyth þat lordyng;
<small>lord to acquaint him with the emperor.</small> Hyt ys worshyp to þe." 966
The kyng of Galys seyde þan,
"So grete a lord ys þer non,
Ȝn alle Crystyante." 969
<small>He agreed, and she bade him ride with his knights to meet that great lord.</small> "Now, swete syr, what-euur be-tyde,
A-ȝayn þat grete lord ȝe ryde,
And alle þy knyȝtys wyth þe." 972

¹ MS. wat.   ² MS. Wax.   ³ R. lorde.

(82)

Emare thaw3te her sone 3ynge,		Emaré taught her son that if
A-3eyn þe emperour komynge,		
How þat he sholde done:	975	
"Swete sone, yn alle þyng,		
Be redy wyth my lord þe kyng,		
And be my swete sone!	978	
When þe emperour kysseth þy fadur[1] so fre,		
Loke 3yf he wylle kysse the,		the emperor kissed him,
A-bowe þe to hym sone;	981	he should say, "Come speak with Emaré, that was put into the sea."
And bydde hym come speke wyth Emare,		
That was putte yn-to þe see,		
Hym-self 3af þe dome."	984	

(83)

Now kometh þe emperour of pryse;		Now the king
A-3eyn hym rode þe kyng of Galys,		
Wyth fulle mykulle pryde.	987	
The chyld was worþy vnþur wede,		and the child with him rode to meet the emperor,
A[2] satte vpon a nobylle stede,		
By hys fadyr syde;	990	
And when he mette þe emperour,		
He valed hys hode wyth gret honour,		
And kyssed hym yn þat tyde;	993	and was kissed by him and other great lords.
And oþur lordys of gret valowre,		
They also kessed Segramowre;		
In herte ys not to hyde.	996	

(84)

The emperours hert[3] anamered gretlye,		The emperor greatly loved the child.
Of þe chylde þat rode hym by,		
Wyth so louely chere.	999	
Segramowre, he s[t]ayde hys stede,		Segramowre, in the hearing of his father and other lords,
Hys owene fadur[4] toke good hede,		
And oþur lordys þat þer were.	1002	
The chylde spake to þe emperour,		
And sayde, "Lord, for þyn honour,		bade the emperor
My worde þat þou wylle here:	1005	

[1] R. fadyr.   [2] R. And; G. A[nd]. *See note on this line.*
[3] R. herte.   [4] R. fadyr.

32 Emaré's Father, Husband, and Son rejoice together.

come speak with his daughter Emaré.
Ʒe shulle come speke wyth Emare,
That changede her name to Egare,
   That was þy powȝþur dere." 1008

(85)

The emperor grew pale, and asked why he was reminded of his sorrow;
The emperour wax alle pale,
And sayde, "Sone, why vmbraydest me of bale,
   And þou may se no bote?" 1011
"Syr, and ȝe wylle go wyth me,
I shalle þe brynge wyth þat lady fre,
   þat ys louesom on to loke." 1014

but was reassured, and went with the child to meet the lady.
Neuur-þe-lesse, wyth hym he wente;
A-ȝeyn hym come þat lady gent,
   Walkynge on her fote. 1017
And þe emperour a-lyȝte þo,
And toke her yn hys armes two,
   And clypte and kyssed her sote. 1020

(86)

There was a
Ther was a joyfulle metynge
Of þe emperour and of þe kynge,
   And also of Emare; 1023

joyful reunion,
And so þer was of Syr [S]egramour,
That aftyr was emperour;
   A fulle gode man was he. 1026

and a great feast was given.
A grette feste þer was holde,
Of erles and barones bolde,
   As testymonyeth þys story. 1029

This is one of the old lays of Britain.
Thys ys on of Brytayne layes,
That was vsed by olde dayes,
   Men callys "playn þe garye."[1] 1032

Jesus, bring us to Thy perpetual glory.
Iheso,[2] þat settes yn þy trone,
So graunte vs wyth þe to w[o]ne,[3]
   In þy perpetualle glorye! Amen.[4] 1035

Explicit Emare.

---

[1] Playn[t] þ' E-garye? *See note on the line.*
[2] R. Jhesu.   [3] MS. wene.
[4] R. *omits* Amen *and* Explicit Emare.

NOTES.

1/1-12. THE longest introductory prayer in any English romance. The Thornton *Morte Arthure* comes next with 11 lines. The explanation (13-18) seems to be unique.

1/3. Probably þat should be omitted as Gough (G.) suggests (*On the Middle English Metrical Romance of Emaré*, Kiel, 1900, p. 37). Cf. *Duke Rowlande and Sir Ottuell of Spayne* (*Eng. Charl. Rom.*, Part II): '"God," he said, "þat alle schall dighte & dele" (490); "—godde þat diede on rode þat atte schall deme & dighte" (1268-69); "I vowe to god þou schall a-bye, þat atte schalle deme & dele"' (1316-17). The three attributes alluded to are the powers of governing, apportioning, and judging. In l. 42, Arthur has the power to apportion gifts and govern; in l. 826, these terms are applied to alms-giving.

1/6. On the genitive without ending, cf. G. (*Dissertation*, p. 7). It is impossible to say whether this usage is due to minstrel or scribe.

1/7. Probably þy should be omitted (G., following Holthausen, *Dissertation*, p. 37).

1/9. One of the numerous conventionalisms in which the romances, especially those written in the tail-rhyme stanzas, abound. About 140 lines of *Emaré* are found elsewhere, often identical, sometimes with slight changes. The number of romances in which the same expression occurs (often more than once in several) is sometimes nearly 20, and rarely less than 5. I have collected repetitions, to the extent of many hundreds, of conventional phrases in the text; but as limited space will not admit the complete list, I quote them only when they have some peculiar interest. Collections may be found in editions of various romances by Kölbing, Zupitza, Zielke and others. A detailed study of this subject might throw light on the relationships of various members of the different "schools" of romance-makers, which I believe existed in mediæval England.

1/14. *euery a*. Originally, doubtless, *ylke a*. Cf. ll. 114, 166.

1/16-17. *sholde—speke*. Here as elsewhere G. emends to avoid hiatus; but I am not sure how far this offended the minstrel's ear. I have noticed 36 cases of its occurrence, and 13 others which are doubtful. In ll. 16, 17, 275, 302, 437, 611, 743, it is avoided by adding an -*n*, thus giving the poem a more pronouncedly Midland character; in ll. 41, 65, 380, 725 (identical), 35, 113, 481, 581, 666, 740, 914 it occurs in connection with a pause in the sense, and was therefore perhaps not felt; in 18 other cases, noted under the different lines, it may be avoided by some slight change or addition. But the popular character of these *rime couée* romances leads me to think that all such improvements, unless warranted by other MSS., are too arbitrary to be of much use.

2/25-27. The title *emperour* suggests the seven versions in which the father is the head of the Holy Roman Empire; but the name

Artyus was probably introduced because *lays* were usually associated with it. But cf. M.A. 275-76.

2/31. Perhaps: "Hé had wéddedde á lady." For a varying pronunciation of *lady*, cf. ll. 476, 632, 638.

2/33. Walrus-tusks were made up into articles of household furniture as early as King Alfred's time (cf. Alfred's *Orosius*, I, 1).

2/34. G. conjectures the Byzantine *Eirene* (*Dissertation*, p. 31). The most famous Irene was Empress of Constantinople, contemporary with Charlemagne, whom there was talk of her marrying. Her son Constantine VI was also thought of for Charlemagne's daughter Rotrud (Gibbon, *op. cit.*, V, 294). But the name Erayne is possibly corrupted from Elayne (Hélène), who was widely connected with the story through *La Belle Hélène de Constantinople*. According to Trivet and in *La Manekine*, she was the heroine's cousin, the senator's wife. Or perhaps Erayne = Igraine, Uther's wife, Arthur's mother.

2/36. "So cúrtays" or "curtáys lady was nóne," or "So cúrtays lády was nóne"? Cf. ll. 40, 64, 74, and 31, 71, 197, 476, 632, 638.

2/37. G. best[e].

2/49-50. The only other case of identical rhyme is easily emended (934-35). Perhaps here we should read *corne* or *korne* for *borne* (50). Cf. "þat was so comly corn" (*Amis*, 1431; cf. also 1950, 2220); "þat riche was & comly korne" (*Duke Rowlande and Sir Ottuell of Spayne*, 1193); "þe beste knyȝt y-core" (*Sir Ferumbras*, 766).

2/53. G. lōrd[e].

2/55. G. adds [sō]; but *fayr* seems to be dissyllabic at times, cf. ll. 163, 197, 437, and especially l. 403 which resembles l. 55.

2/57. *Abro* = Abra, probably the mediæval Latin word for *female servant*, translated in 15th century glosses (Wright, *A.S. and O.E. Vocabularies*, 1884, I, 623/22; 691/40) as *bowre-mayde, burwoman*. The word was known to Ælfric (*op. cit.*, index), perhaps through the Septuagint (cf. also *Du Cange*). More remotely it is Greek ("Αβρα or 'Αβρα), but supposed to come from an Oriental source (Sophocles in his lexicon gives a Chaldean equivalent).

In the sense of *handmaid*, it was perhaps given to Abra, daughter of St. Hilaire, Bishop of Poitiers (*Hist. Lit. de la France*, I, Pt. II, 140, 142, 154); but scarcely to the Saracen princess, sister of the sultan of Babylon (*Amadis of Greece*, Pt. II, ch. 1 ff.). I supposed that it might have come direct from Arabic (on the hypothesis of a Spanish or Portuguese original for *Amadis*); but in this language *Abla*, a common name for women meaning *she-camel*, and familiar through the heroine of the ancient Bedouin romance of *Antar*, seems to be the nearest counterpart. Still, the corruption of Abla into Abra is imaginable. Further, an Abda is mentioned by Amari (*Storia dei Musulmani di Sicilia*, Firenze, 1854-72, II, 448, with note 5) as the name of a Fatemite princess of Egypt, who died about the end of the 10th century, possessed of great treasure, including "Sicilian robes." But for the curious coincidence I should not have mentioned this name, the other derivation being more likely.

As to the meaning of the presence of the name in *Emaré*, I am in doubt. The nurse or "mistress" of the heroine appears in a comparatively small group of versions, and is usually nameless (Clarissa or Beatrix in *Hélène*, Benigna in *Mai*). The only hypothesis that I can suggest is, that in the French, Abra or a similar Oriental name was connected with the magic cloth (perhaps the "amerayle dowȝter" was so called); and that the English minstrel, knowing the Latin *abra* (perhaps from the Septuagint, perhaps from glosses similar to those in Wright), transferred it, as he might suppose correctly, to the person whose station it indicated.

3/58 ff. But Trivet's Constance learned the seven sciences and various tongues (*op. cit.* p. 5). For the learned heroine, cf. *Le Bone Florence of Rome* (58–63, and MS. fr. 24384, fol. 203 b), *Guy of Warwick* (80–92). In *Partonopeus de Blois* (Crapelet, 1834, 4572–4614, and Buckley, Roxburghe Club, 1862, 3204–27) she studies until she masters the art of magic.

3/72. G. omits *we*.

3/77. *weddewede*. In the *Wars of Alexander*, 5089, 1558, *Morte Arthure*, 950, 4285, is the form *wedowe*, which would give *wedowhede*.

3/78. This line evidently alludes to the emperor's licentious character. The abrupt change of subject, and the broken rhyme-scheme hint at an omission of some matter. Cf. note on l. 187.

3/79. G. Sōnę [þēr-]after, to avoid hiatus.

3/80. G. kyngę [o͞ut] of, to avoid hiatus and inorganic -e.

3/82–83. The school of Palermo was famous throughout Europe under the rule of the Normans, who fostered Mussulman work there. After the Sicilian Vespers, the workmen spread their art through Italy, and thence into all parts of Europe.

3/83. G. worþylsę was.

3/85. Perhaps: " Syr Térgaunte hýʒte þat nóbylle knyʒt." The usual forms of the name are Tervagant and Termagant, the latter a corruption (cf. Skeat, note on Chaucer, B 2000, and Ritson, *Anc. Eng. Metr. Rom.*, III, 257 ff., for quotations and discussion). Common as are the two latter forms (cf. especially *Bevis of Hampton*, index), referring always to a Saracen deity, I have not found *Tergaunte* elsewhere. But this Tergaunte is apparently a Christian king whose father conquered the Sultan of Babylon (cf. *Introduction*, p. xxxi, n. 5, and note on l. 158 ff. below).

3/86–88. The connection seems to be: presented . . . with, l. 87 being parenthetical. L. 86. G. [a-]ryght. L. 88. G. clōth[e].

4/91. Perhaps: and [of] rubyes. Cf. l. 139. *Topaze*. Supposed to have the power to keep water from boiling, to cool men's passions and to kill toads (Pannier, *Les Lapidaires Français*, Paris, 1882, index). *Rubyes*. Mentioned only by the supposititious Mandeville, who gives them a chief place, as conferring favour and love, curing sick animals, and generally comforting the wearer's heart (Pannier, *op. cit.*).

4/94. *crapowtes*. Not mentioned by the French lapidaries. Cf. N. E. D. *Crapaud, Crapautee* for other quotations. It occurs in the Northern romance *Thomas of Erceldoune* (52). *nakette*. Perhaps (n)achate, as Dr. Murray also suggests. The text shows a tendency to write e for a, as: cledde, wesh, wes; but *Destruction of Troy* has *achates*, *Wars of Alexander, acats*. Or, the word may be some derivative (perhaps corrupted) from *nacre* = mother-of-pearl. There is also a rare stone *echite*, but this is more remote phonetically. Cf. also *Godefroi* under *nace* = cloth of gold.

4/97. G. clōth [hyt].

4/103. G. The empero͞ur [þan].

4/113. *asowr.* Cf. *N. E. D.* for quotations. The colour seems to have been greatly beloved in the Middle Ages.

4/116. G. clōth[e].

4/118. Cf. *Sir Gawayne*, l. 613 : "As mony burde þer-aboute had ben seue*n* wynter i*n* toune."

5/122. G. [Dāme] Idoyne. Perhaps Ydoÿne? But the word is a dissyllable in *Cursor Mundi* (20) and Gower's *Confessio Amantis* (VI, 879), where the romance is mentioned ; also in *Sir Degrevant* (1477-78), where the tale is said to have been represented on the tapestry of a bed. The story seems to have originated in England in the 12th century (*An English Miscellany*, Oxford, 1901, p. 386 ff.); but the English romance *Sir Amadas* (*Amadace*) borrows nothing but the hero's name from the French.

5/125. *trewe-loue flour.* Herb Paris (Paris Quadrifolia), similar to trillium. The setting of its four leaves was supposed to resemble a true-love knot. Cf. *Sir Degrevant* (1032, 1039, 1484) ; the *Awntyrs off Arthure* (354, 510) ; *Sir Gawayne* (612) ; *Rauf Coilȝear* (473). Here the flower seems to have been used to help the love-charm in the magic robe.

5/127. *carbunkulle.* Supposed to shine with a red light in darkness. *safere.* Good for the general health, especially diseases of the eyes, head and tongue, a safe-guard against poverty, prison, and the machinations of enemies (Pannier, *op. cit.*).

5/128. *Kassydonys.* Its qualities are given vaguely as contributing to health and prosperity. Cf. *casydoynes* (*Cleanness*, 1471), *calcydoyne* (*Pearl*, 1002) ; also *calcidoynes, Wars of Alexander* (5274). *onyx.* An evil stone which brings bad dreams and strife (Pannier, *op. cit.*).

5/130. *Deamondes.* Especially prized for the working of enchantment and against enchantment by others (Pannier, *op. cit.*).

5/132. *And.* Possibly repeated from l. 131. Qy. Sing? Cf. note on l. 151 below.

5/134. *Trystram and Isowde.* From the 12th century on, one of the most influential of romances. Here the forms of the names seem to be English (cf. *Cursor Mundi*, 17).

5/136. G. [a-]ryght.

5/137-44. These lines, almost identical with 89-96, may have been copied twice by mistake ; but the detail suits the context here better than in stanza 8, hence, I judge that they may have been used there in place of lost matter giving more account of Tergaunte.

5/146. This romance, arising in the 12th century, was almost as popular as the two preceding ; and like them was early known in England, even if it did not actually originate there.

5/151. *knyȝtus and senatowres.* Possibly here as in l. 131 the pattern suddenly intrudes upon the materials ; but names of stones are expected. If the poem was at any time taken down from hearing, the line might have been corrupted from "Ther wer onyx and centaureus," which would rhyme correctly with *vertues.* My authority for *centaureus* is Heinrich von Neustadt (quoted by Smith, *Shakespeare's Pericles and Apollonius of Tyre*, Philadelphia, 1898, pp. 75-76) ; the nearest that Pannier gives is *ceraunus.* The plant, *centaurus*, was well known.

5/152. The "vertues" of emeralds were supposed to foretell the

Notes. Pages 6, 7, lines 154–188.

future, cure tertian fever, bring wealth, protect in battle, storm and lightning, cool the passions, strengthen the sight, give eloquence, etc.

6/154. *Koralle.* Protects against storm and lightning, increases crops, and chases devils.

6/155. *Perydotes.* Supposed to be a protection at night against devils and bad dreams. *crystalle.* Valued for its use in lighting fire, and supposed to increase nurses' milk. (Pannier, *op. cit.*)

6/156. *garnettes.* See *N. E. D.* for origin and quotations of this word. Not mentioned by the French lapidaries.

6/157. *oon.* G. was [þēr] ōōn. Cf. *Dissertation*, p. 41, note on l. 157, for this use of *one*. But perhaps we should read *don*. Cf. *made* (121) and *dyght* (133).

6/158 ff. The "sowdan" of Babylon was a familiar figure in English romances of the 14th century. Cf. especially the two redactions of *Fierabras*, known as *Sir Ferumbras* and the *Sowdone of Babylone;* also, the southern *Octavian*, in which he is said to have conquered "Gales and Spayne" among other lands (907 ff.); in the northern *Octavian* also, the "sowdan" is presumably of Babylon. The allusion is not, of course, to the city of that name, but vaguely to the Orient, according to Graf (*op. cit.* 4, 552), to the sovereigns Ajubidi of Egypt and Syria (cf. *Archivio . . . di Storia Patria*, IV, 552). Undoubtedly the passage alludes to some romance, perhaps of the *Guillaume d'Orange* cycle, influenced by the Crusades. In *Foulque de Candie* (by Herbert le Duc, *circ.* 1170) the hero loves a Saracen princess who gives him a sleeve embroidered with gems, and also conquers the Sultan of Babylon. The poem called *Tancré* I have not been able to find. Again, Richard Cœur de Lion (in the English romance) fights with Saladin at Babylon and there wins much treasure.

6/162. *testymoyeth.* "Si con l'escriture tesmoigne" (*La Mule sans Frein*, 885), "Si com tiesmogne li escris" (Mouskes, 18695), and elsewhere. The line is almost certainly translated, as is l. 1029. The verb, which I have not seen elsewhere, looks like a hybrid of *testifies* and *tesmoigner*, or else is formed from the noun *testimony*. *Sir Gowther* (309) doubtless translates the same expression: "þo testamentys þus þei sey."

6/163–64. A maiden was supposed to be able to tame the unicorn. The two are represented, also with flowers and birds, on a 15th century tapestry in the Musée de Cluny at Paris.

6/168. On the extensive use of "ymagerye" in Sicilian work, cf. *Introduction*, p. xxxi, with n. 1. Romances, legends of saints, historic characters were attempted.

6/170. *sone.* Qy. *sone* or *soon*? Cf. ll. 158, 173.

6/175. G. grēt[e] loue.

6/176. *in specyalte.* Perhaps, as in Barbour's *Bruce* (VII, 246), the sense is, in special liking or partiality.

6/181–82. I see no reason for the optative here. Perhaps we should read þar or þor(e) and wor(e) (also in 721–22) as in 832–33, this last being singular=was, as it is still used in Mid-Yorkshire to-day.

6/182. G. lóng[e]. Cf. ll. 355, 364, 718. This causes hiatus.

6/184. G. wolde [hōm hym] wénde.

6/185. léue át. Hiatus.

7/187–88. *Kvng* evidently refers to Tergaunte, and l. 188 has been corrupted by introducing the word *emperour* to show the change of subject. This breaking of the thought between the seventh and eighth lines may be a sign that the robe passage (78-187) has been foisted in from another source. This may have been a longer version of the same story (*Mai* describes an azure samite, set with gold and precious stones, and a magic robe appears in many versions and kindred folk-tales). The character of the passage bears out this hypothesis : it is altogether out of scale for a lay, but can be paralleled by many descriptive passages in romances, French and English, particularly the former; it contains more than a tenth part of the poem, but is mechanical and full of repetitions, as if the author had remembered but imperfectly, and so was thrown upon his own invention, which was not great (cf. the robe passage in *Erec et Enide* (6735-809), which is on a similar plan and scale).

7/195. G. forth [þan].

7/200. G. gö[e]th. But *goth* is a common spelling in the N.E. Midlands, though here it makes the line short.

7/201. *chare.* This vehicle is mentioned frequently and much earlier than the quotations given in *N. E. D.* (cf. *Kyng of Tars*, 339, 354, and for a long description of a hunting-chare, *Squire of Low Degree*, 739 ff.).

7/210. Li3te óf. Hiatus.

7/211. Qy. both [vp-]on?

7/211-12. Probably fǭtę—swǭtę (cf. 1017, 1020), as G. suggests; otherwise, we have seven successive e-rhymes.

8/223-24. G. paraphrases, according to *Amis*, 571-2, but this is unnecessary. In *Sir Degarre* (Auchinleck MS. 827-28) we find :

"That all his herte and his thout,
Hire to loue was i-browt."

8/226. *an-amored.* The word seems rare until much later. *N. E. D.* quotes Robert of Brunne (8170) and Chaucer (*L. G. W.*, 1606).

8/229. *metewhyle.* I have not found this word elsewhere ; but *Morte Arthure* gives *mette-while* (3903) = measured, *i. e.* little while ; and also *mette* = mete (2491).

8/239. *Popus Bullus.* Cf. *Powlus Pystolus* and *Parabolus of Solamon* (*Degrevant*, 1438-39). Possibly, attempts at Latinization without knowledge of the language, perhaps to give a learned effect, but more probably to be regarded only as W. Midland endings.

Here the Pope's assent is taken for granted ; elsewhere, he is bribed by help against the Saracens, and then consents only because it is revealed to him in a vision that no harm shall come.

8/244. " And whén vpón' her hýt was dón," improves the rhythm.

8/245-46. She seemed untainted by earth, that is, supernatural in her beauty. Cf. G. (*Dissertation*, 37-39) on a possible mythological significance for the robe.

8/251. G. omits *syr.*

9/261. G. 3ōu [ay], but 3ou [now] would be more to the point.

9/264. *þhorne.* An indication that þ was little more than d or t for the scribe. In other cases: s(h)uch (702), she s(he)wed (730), w(h)esshen (890), the proximity of an h may have led to its repetition.

9/265. Qy. right[e] (adverb) ?

9/266. G. [myʒtȳ] ōthę. But cf. *Degrevant* (193–94):
"Than the eorl wax worth (= wroth)
And swore many a gret owth."
grete is probably right, notwithstanding the hiatus.

9/270. G. [rȳche], to avoid repetition of *nobulle* (268). Cf. ll. 590, 644.

9/271–72. *drynke*. Cf. *Amis and Amiloun*, drink (2191) rhyming with lesing (2192), with lesing-þing-king (1587-90-93-96), with þing (1666–67), with þing-ʒing-wepeing (1707-10-13-16). For dryng = drink, cf. *ibid.*, ed. Kölbing, p. xxi; for thing = think (seem), and thinke = thing (object) cf. Robson, *Three Metrical Romances*, index.

9/273. *shate*. Cf. *Ayenbite of Inwit*, ssat (45). The form is rare but a correct development of O.E. *scēat*.

9/275. G. Wyth-ōwte[n].

9/278. G. [fer] frō. Cf. ll. 349, 353 suggest that *boot* was long enough to stand for a metrical unit itself; l. 674 contains an inorganic -e.

9/280. Qy. hym [vm] be-þowght? Cf. *Isumbras*, l. 426, *Eglamour*, l. 73, *Towneley Plays*, 5/123, *Ywaine*, l. 1583, *Alexius* (598).

9/281. *hadde alle*. Hiatus. Qy. hadde [hyt]?

10/287. G. And tōkę [hym] *up* [full] hāstylȳ. The line scans, as it is, though anapæstic.

10/295. G. aʒeyn[es]. Qy. *a-ʒeijn*, or *wrowghte*, with hiatus? The former reads better.

10/298. *lasshed*. In this sense the word seems peculiarly Northern. Cf. *York Plays* (xxxi, 10, xlvi, 37), *Cleanness* (707), *Morte Arthure* (2801, 1459), *Destruction of Troy* (6789). In Jamison, the word has similar meanings, and, according to the quotation, also in the *Mid-Yorks. Glossary*, although Clough Robinson makes a special application of it.

10/307. G. They sowʒt her, etc.

11/326. Practically the same time as in *La Manekine*, where the heroine drifted from Hungary to Berwick (eight days, l. 1168), and from Berwick to Rome (twelve days, 4761). According to Trivet, she was first three, and then five years at sea (*Originals and Analogues*, pp. 13, 39).

11/329. *ʒarked ʒore*. The idea here is probably *ordained*. The word *ʒarked* occurs repeatedly in *Cleanness* (652, 758, 1708), *Wars of Alexander* (114, 2449, 4894), in *Destruction of Troy* (414, 5595, 10738, 11265, etc.), sometimes from O.E. *gearcian* = to prepare, sometimes from a word akin to the modern *jerk*, meaning, to rain upon, as blows.

11/335. G. thurstę *and* hunger, which reads much better. The phrase is repeated in l. 683.

11/338. *Galys*. G. (*Dissertation*, 31–32) sums up the evidence for Wales and Galicia. This form occurs, alike for each country, with the accent on either syllable. The attempt to connect the poem with the Arthur cycle suggests that the French author intended Wales, while the English minstrel may have translated Galicia, through the popularity of St. James of Compostella, to whom there are many allusions in 14th century literature. But for an additional reason favouring Galicia, see note on l. 481 ff.

11/342. *Kadore*. Cadwr, Cadeir, son of Geraint map Erbin, mentioned in a triad, was Arthur's sword-bearer (*Romania*, xxx, 11–13).

40   *Notes. Pages* 11–14, *lines* 348–436.

Mouskes (21009 ff.) mentions an historic Kados (= Cadoc, also Kadore), Seigneur of Gaillon (in Normandy, but suggestive of Gaille = Galles = Gaule), who was prominent at the battle of Bouvines (1212), and may have suggested the introduction of this name into the *lai*.

11/348.   *le.* Perhaps *shore* as in *Destruction of Troy* (2806).

12/349 ff.   Cf. G. (*Emaré*, p. 36, note on 349 seq.) for an interesting emendation of this stanza; but the participle in *and* is not warranted. Cf. on l. 793 below.

12/352.   went[e] forth [vp-]on? G. went forth [up-]on.

12/360.   Only in *La Manekine* is the change of name emphasized as here. There also the two names *Joie* and *Manekine* have meanings. This idea is carried further in *Emaré*. In the concealment of origin, the influence of the Swan-maiden stories appears, in the opening that it affords for a false accusation.

12/363.   Qy. hom[e] or (G.) hōm [hē]? Cf. l. 708.

12/365.   Cf. *Havelok*, ll. 1022, 1821, 1843, 1882 for this use of the word. I have not found the simile elsewhere.

12/371.   G. myȝht[en].   Qy. myȝt[e]?

13/387.   *Wyth* = in company with, or in honour of?

13/391 ff. That this detail was in the original is suggested by *La Filla de l'Emperadar Contasti* (*Romania*, xxx, 528):

"*E* lo rey . . . menga molt volente*r*, e la donzella lo servi molt cortesament al mils q*ue* ella poch, e lo rey se pres molt esme*nt* del gran servey q*ue* la donzella feya e de la sua bellesa e de les sucs fayssons qui era*n* tant plasents e tan humils."

13/392. *kurtulle.* Evidently both this and the surcoat were made of the magic cloth. The allusion to the child's kirtle (848) seems to be a reflection of this passage.

13/397.   G. kyng [hē].

13/398.   So fáyr a ladý he sýȝ neuu*r* nón), or, So fáyr a lády he sýȝ neuu*r* nón),' or, So fáyr a ladý he syȝ néuu*r* nón)?

14/415.   Cf. G. (*Dissertation*, p. 43). The phrase is too common in 14th and 15th century works to need special quotation. The stuff was evidently fashionable. Cf. note on l. 430.

14/422 f. This applies more nearly to *La Comtesse d'Anjou*, in which the steward (constable) did send for the heroine to teach his children (not "courtesy" but needlework). Why Kadore makes up this story, I fail to see.

14/428. *be.* Optative, perhaps to qualify the very strong statement.

14/430. Probably, as also 451, corrupted from 415. Ray = *rei*, king, and "ryche ray" = *riche rei*, occur commonly in earlier works, as *Sir Perceval of Galles*, the *Awntyrs off Arthure*, and others; also *ray* is found in the *Towneley Plays*, *Wars of Alexander*, etc., but *roy* in the *Morte Arthure*, *Torrent of Portyngale*, etc.

14/433.   G. [full] verament. But *verament* is usually unmodified. The line is short, unless *kyng* was written with an inorganic -e, or the pause represented a syllable.

14/434.   Aftyr hýs modýr he sént, or, módyr he sént?

14/436.   G. browȝt[e] forth [full] hāstelȳ.

Notes. Pages 14–16, lines 439–504.

14/439. G. The clŏth [up-]on, etc.

14/440. G. [y-]dyght. Cf. l. 395.

14/441. *And* is perhaps superfluous ; the line is seemingly appositive with *she*, perhaps with *being* understood.

14/443. G. I sawę neuer [anȳ] wommon. The implication was that she was a fairy. Cf. *Mai*, col. 60, ll. 5–7.

15/458 ff. Usually the feast is described at length (notably in *La Manekine*, ll. 2153–2361). Cf. also other romances, *Squire Low Deg.*, 313–26, *Morte Arthure*, 176–238, *Rauf Coilȝear*, 183–221. The brevity here shows how out of proportion is the passage concerning the robe.

15/461. G. Dūkę [and]. But the line is conventional as it stands. Possibly the -e was silent and the pause filled the foot. Cf. *La Manekine*, 2365 ff. :

"Li rois est demourés arrier,
Et avoeques li sa moillier.
Tant s'entraiment andui de cuér," etc.

15/472. G. Moch[e].

15/479. G. (note on l. 479), following Morsbach, Conceyued[e]. From parallel cases, I should read *Conceiȝued*.

16/481 ff. The King of France may be Charlemagne, and the allusion to his wars in Spain (cf. note on l. 158 ff.), but I think not. I have given reasons in the *Introduction* for holding that the French lay arose in the first half of the 13th century. In 1212 occurred the last great Saracenic attempt upon Europe. The King of Castile, hard pressed by the Moors, sent abroad for help, especially to France, in that his daughter Blanche had married Louis VIII. At the battle of Tolosa the Moors were utterly routed, and all Christendom rejoiced. Such an event must have influenced poetic imaginations long after, perhaps the more so because at this very period Carolingian traditions (which deal so largely with Saracenic wars) were deliberately fostered (Petite Dutaillis, *Louis VIII*, Paris, 1894, 12–14). After some time, the King of France would naturally become the chief personage (perhaps through reflection from Charlemagne), and Galicia might replace Castile as being more familiar. A degree of support is given to this hypothesis by the facts that in *La Filla de l'Emperador Contasti*, the husband is King of Castile ; and in *Mai*, the king's uncle is King of Castile and oppressed by Saracens (col. 99 ff.).

16/484. [He] sente ? Ll. 483–84–85 all begin with *And*. G. After þe kyng sentę of Galȳs.

16/494. G. sent[e].

16/495. Cf. note on l. 461.

16/496. G. st[e]ward [hē]. But perhaps *st[e]ẃard* alone would suffice, *w* being vocalic, as in *Havelok*, 281, 453, 1144,.etc. ; *Pearl*, 821, 830, 942, and elsewhere.

16/499. G. yn [þylke] plāce. If *yn place* can bear the meaning "as it was her place to do," the short line must be emended differently, perhaps *wente* [þan].

16/503. A fáyr chýld borne and a gódelé.

16/504. *Kyngus marke.* In *Havelok* (604, 2139–47) the hero had on his right shoulder a cross which shone like a carbuncle at night. In *La Filla del Rey di Dacia:* "una rosetta la quale egli avea nella gola, che nacque con essa" (Wesselofsky, p. 32). Here, a double crown? In several versions, the union of the two kingdoms, France and England, by this marriage is emphasized (notably, *Yst, Faz*).

16/505. "They crýstẹned hýt," reads better.

16/506. G. And hym called, etc.

16/511. G yn [grēt] hȳȝyngẹ. From the repetition of *hyt* in three successive lines, I judge that l. 511 may have read: "He wrouȝte [þe lett*ur*]," etc.

17/523. G. hym ȝaf. Qy. ȝaf [to], or ȝaf[e]?

17/524. The same sum paid in *La Manekine* (*quarante sols*, 3060). Read foẅrty? Cf. note on l. 496.

17/532. G. letter [þan].

17/538. G. " Heddes thrē hē hadde thērẹ."

17/539. The most monstrous creation in any version. In *La Manekine*, it had four feet and was hideous to look upon.

17/540. *feltred.* This occurs in *Cleanness* (224), *Morte Arthure* (1078), *Sir Gowther* (74, 748), *Towneley Plays* (377/318, 102/65), and in *Mid-Yorks. Glossary* to-day, meaning clotted.

18/554. G. kyng [full], and omits *full* from l. 555.

18/557. G. That euer ȝ man [y-]bōr[e]n was. Qy. That éu*ur* mán y bōr[e]n wás?

18/572. G. " Her tō serue[n] at her wyllẹ."

18/575. The messenger's journey was entirely by land, and according to Trivet, "der Büheler" and others, the old queen's castle seems to have been mid-way in a two-days' journey. This geography is reasonable only in the case of Trivet, as "der Büheler" places the court at London.

19/582. G. Þat raftẹ hym, etc.

19/585. G. In fȳrẹ.

19/588. *towne.* A word often on the lips of minstrels of the market-place.

19/598-99. "The méssengér ‖ knéwë no gýle,
But ródë hóm ‖ móny a mýle."

19/606. *de*[*l*]*fulle.* Warranted by *Cursor Mundi* (MS. Fairfax, 768), *Sir Gawayne* (560), *Roberd of Cysyle* (Utterson, p. 14), *Cleanness* (400), etc.; but *Cath. Anglic.* gives also *drefulle = terribilis.*

19/607. *stode yn.* Hiatus. G. stōdẹ yn [hys].

19/608. *swonynge.* Probably *sowenynge*, cf. l. 284.

20/616. G. [þēr] bē.

20/625. G. [þan] saydẹ.

20/628. Loke [þat], etc.?

20/632. He is ashamed on me, a simple lady, is the construction.

20/635. So in *Dacia* (pp. 18-19) : "ella non puote quasi essere più gentile donna ch'ella èe, nè meglio nata."

20/639. *hond*[*e*]. The scribe wrote the abbreviation of what was perhaps to him the more familiar plural.

21/652-54. This description of costume seems peculiar to *Emaré.* It suggests a time when short surcoats were the fashion, but long surcoats were still remembered. From its explanatory character, I judge that it may have been an addition by the English minstrel.

Notes. Pages 21-23, lines 655-732.

21/655. G. a-fēr[e]dẹ. Also in l. 698.

21/657. G. chýldẹ [un]tŏ.

21/660. Cf. Büh (3047). " Das das schiff nam manigen stosz."

21/661. G. chýld [by-]gan. Cf. l. 727.

21/661 ff. Curiously enough, Gower's version is the only other in which this detail occurs. Cf. ll. 1078-81:

> "And tho sche tok hire child in honde
> And yaf it sowke, and evere among
> Sche wepte, and otherwhile song
> To rocke with hire child aslepe."

But it is probable, in the absence of other close correspondences, that the two descriptions are independent of each other.

21/669. The emendation *on grōwf* is admissible as far as rhymes go (cf. 219-222-225-228); but seems unnecessary. The form growth may be the *gruȝt* of *Cleanness* (810) from *grucchen* (= usually *complain* but there *accost*). But in Mid-Yorks. to-day there is a preterite *gruot*, of which in this MS. *growht* may be a corruption.

22/685-87. In the versions in which the second flight is to Rome, the rescuer is often a senator, sometimes the Pope or a cardinal. In *La Belle Hélène* he is called Joseran, a name which might have been corrupted to Iurdan; but the exile whom he and his wife receive is the princess Plaisance, whose sufferings form a parallel to those of the heroine. According to Enikel and Büheler, as in *Emaré*, he is a burgess.

22/688-89. Cf. 343-44. G. Eụuẹrȳ [mornyng].

22/691. G. þ[ylke].

22/692. G. [wāter-]sȳdẹ. Possibly [Tiber] as this river is mentioned in *Mai*, *Enikel* and *La Manekine*—all fairly closely related to *Emaré*.

22/694. Does *by þe brymme* mean by the shore, or by the sea? In the sense of torrent, flood, it occurs in *Sir Gawayne* (2172), *Cleanness* (365), *Wars of Alexander* (4080), seemingly in a Northern usage. This passage is uncertain, but ll. 352-53 suggest that the boat was *on* the shore, therefore *by* the sea. But the other interpretation is usually given.

22/697. G. The clōth [up-]on.

22/700. G. [a-]ryght. Or, þouȝt[e]?

22/704. "Lórd," she saýde, " y hette Égarýe."

23/715. G. What þat [euer]. Or, Whát [so] þát she wýlle cráue?

23/716. G. hyt wyll[e].

23/722. G. mēte[s]. But cf. 7/218, 13/401, and note on l. 181 above.

23/723. Cf. *La Manekine* (6403): "Tout a son voloir a esté."

23/727. G. [Segramōur] by-gan, both for the rhythm and to avoid repetition of *child*.

23/731. G. nor[i]tōwre = curtesye and thewe, l. 38.

23/732. So in *Mai*, she had not laughed in eight years; and in *La Manekine* (6267-72):

"Mais onques une fois n'i rist,
Ne un mot de canchon n'i dist,
Ne ne vesti dras de couleur.
Tousjors en dolour u en pleur
Ou en grieté ou en pensee
Est toute sa vie tornee."

23/733-38. Cf. *Sir Degarre* (273-74):
"Bi that hit was ten ȝer old,
Hit was a fair child, and a bold."

23/737. So *Mai* (col. 196, ll. 25-26):
"dô wart er sô kurtîs
daȝ er an lobe behielt den prîs,"

and ll. 21-22: "man lêrte in ze allen zîten
diu ors schône rîten."

24/742. *cler of vyce.* Perhaps taken directly from the Fr. *à cler vis*. The word *vyce* for face is uncommon, but occurs as *vyse* in *Pearl* (254), *vys* in *Richard Cœur de Lion* (3187, 3406).

24/754. G. [of] aventōwres.

24/757. G. kyng [hē]. Or, [Then] saýde the kýng?

24/764-68. A singular disregard of the usage of *thou* and *ye*. Cf. also ll. 965-66, 971-72, 1005-8.

24/769. G. The kyng þe letter tōke tō rēde.

24/773. Usually, "Allas!" he seide, "that I was boren!" (*Degarre*, 83; similarly, *Havelok*, *Roberd of Cysyle*, and others.) G. euer [on érþe] born ȳ was. "That ý euur bór[e]n wás" introduces less change. Cf. note on l. 557.

25/776. G. Thys letter neuer cōme frō mē.

25/779. The sense is: but for God's will, *i. e.* I must bow to God's will.

25/780. So likewise in *La Manekine* (4259-60).

25/782. And tóke þe kýng vp hástylý.

25/784. G. bōth[e].

25/793. G. [sō ǵent]; but this rhyme with *nd* does not occur in *Emaré*. Qy. þe kynge [*so* or *full* kende]? Cf. *Sege of Melayne* (1437): "Þat wele for kene are kende." In the sense of known, renowned, the word is not uncommon, especially in the North. Kende for kynde = race, family, also occurs, and the line may have read: Þen sayde þe kynge of noble *or* ryche kende. It is tempting to suggest: "'Alas,' þen sayde þe kynge sykende." Then, when the participle became *sykynge*, it might easily have been lost through the repetition of the syllable *kynge*. Cf. note on l. 877, below.

25/797. G. omits *any*.

25/799 ff. The remission of punishment is peculiar to *Emaré*. In *La Manekine* and Enikel's chronicle she is immured; in *Mai* and in Trivet's *Constance*, killed with a sword; in the other chief versions, burned.

25/805. When shé was fléd óuur þe (see) fóme?

26/815. So *Mai* (col. 197, l. 24) "nieman kunde im trôst gegeben."

26/819 ff. *for his sake.* He could not possibly blame himself. The penance is usually, as in *Mai*, *Trivet*, and elsewhere, for killing his mother.

Notes. Pages 26–28, lines 824–878.

26/824. *wordes.* Not uncommon for worldes. *Prompt. Parv.* has wordely = mundanus; *word* occurs in the York Plays, in *Havelok*, in *Wars of Alex.*, *Awntyrs off Arthure*, *Sir Gowther*, and elsewhere.

26/832-34. These details are closely paralleled in *Mai* (col. 203, ll. 35-39).

26/833. G. lust[es]. But *wore* may be singular. Cf. note on ll. 181-82.

26/835. G. salt[e].

27/841 ff. Here Trivet approaches *Emaré* most closely. Cf. "Cist estoit apris priuement de sa mere Constance, qe, quant il irreit a la feste . . . que, totes autres choses lessetz, se meit de-uant le Roi dengleterre, quant il fust assis a manger, pur li seruier; Et que de nule part se remuat hors del regard al Roi, e qe il se afforsat bien & curteisement lui seruir." The heroine's instructions, as far as they go, agree with the *Babees Book* (ed. Furnivall, 1868), much of which was written at about this time.

27/842. G. to here [tō] come. But "to hérë cóme" is possible.

27/847. G. shal[t], and *shalle* may have come by anticipation of *halle;* but it occurs for the second person in the *Sege of Melayne*. Cf. quotation in note on 1/3.

27/850. Lókë, sóne, so curtáys þou bé. Or, Lóke, sóne, two monosyllabic feet with a pause between them.

27/852. Cf. 3/75.

27/856. G. [y-]dōne.

27/864. The only meaning that I can get out of this archaic phrase "lovable or amiable under linen" is that the wearing of linen, instead of the peasants' wool, was once associated with the idea of good manners because only gentlemen could afford linen. The phrase seems to occur chiefly in Northern texts. It is equivalent to "goodly under gore" and "seemly under sark."

27/867. *kowrs.* Plural in idea.

27/871. Then sáydë álle þat lóked hym vpón'. The hiatus could easily be avoided by an -n.

27/873. G. halle[s]. Cf. ll. 898-9, where *halles* should be *halle* to accord. But the minstrel was not troubled by the juxtaposition of the plural and the generalized singular. Cf. ll. 389-90, also 26, 28, 29 ; 94, 142 ; 125-26, 127-28, 149-50, 154-55.

28/874. The kýnge sàydë.

28/876. G. omits *he seyd*. Here again Trivet is very similar: "A ceo le Roi demaunda del Iuuencel son noun ; Et il respondi que son noun fu Moris."

28/877. G. þat [ylke]. Or, The[re upo]n? Or, originally :

"Then þat kynge of noble kende,
Toke vp a grete sykende"?

28/878 ff. *Tókë vp.* Hiatus. So in *La Manekine*, 6017-20 :

"Quant je regardai cest enfant,
D'un mien fil m'alai a pensant,
Que j'euch, bien a passé set ans."

So, *Emaré*, ll. 811-16, suggests *La Manekine* in the length of time, and in the incident of ll. 811-13, which is seemingly generalized, while in the French poem it is his own son playing unrecognized in the senator's hall, who causes his emotion.

28/880. G. adds [anȳ], but the line is conventional as it stands.

28/887. So *La Manekine*, 6003-5 :
"Or me dites voir, biaus dous ostes,
Si cis enfes ichi est vostres."
"Oïl, sire, voir, il est miens."
And Gower (1387): "He seide: Yee, so I him calle."

28/890. W(h)esshen a-ʒéÿn aftyr méte. G. a-ʒeyn [hem]; but the verb is not usually reflexive.

28/893. G. [a-]dōwnẹ.

28/895. G. The kyngẹ þe burgeys callẹd hym tyll.

28/897. *body* in the sense of *person* has been and still is used, especially in the North.

28/901-3. *serued—wente—tellys*. The minstrel does not pay much heed to sequence of tenses. Cf. ll. 200-1, 721-23, 745-46, etc.

28/904. *Soone*. *Son* or *soon?*

28/905. *grete ende*. Cf. l. 917. G. reads *grece ende* (i. e. top of the steps); but the MS. has clearly t. The "great end" of the hand would naturally be the thumb (cf. Italian *dito grosso*, Catalan *dit gros*, English *great toe*).

29/909. Iń the lóndẹ of Galýs, to avoid hiatus.

29/916. G. Tō chāmber when þe kyng shuldẹ wéndẹ.

29/918. G. helpẹ[d].

29/924. A curious synecdoche, which must have arisen in a period when chins were not hidden under wimples.

29/926. G. herd[e].

29/929. This scans with two anapests. *vmbraydest*. This spelling is not uncommon, especially in the Nŏrth. Cf. *R. Mannyng* (3485, 8004), *Cleanness* (1622, but meaning to accost), *Wars of Alexander* (1800), *Destruction of Troy* (9903).

29/935. G. bōth[e] t[h]ō.

30/940. The exclamation is singularly modern; but cf. *Perceval of Galles* (1691), *Amadace* (Robson, 7/9), *Patience* (264), *Pearl* (108, 1148), etc.

30/948. G. tóldẹ. *Y-tolde* is here the preterite representing O.E. *getealde*, not the past participle.

30/950. G. Was [y-]woxen.

30/951. G. And thowʒt [up-]on.

30/968. G. grētẹ a lōrd[yng].

31/979. Almost entirely anapestic.

31/984. G. Hym-self [hē] ʒaf.

31/989. *A* for *he* may be due to the scribe. It occurs in *Wars of Alexander* (4777, and Ashmole MS. only, 1492), in *Sir Ferumbras* passim, and is found in various dialects to-day, including districts of Yorkshire.

31/992. One of the special directions in the *Babees Book*.

31/997. Almost anapæstic.

31/1000. G. (*Dissertation*, p. 3) at first *stayde*, afterwards *say*[*s*]*de*. Perhaps 'sayde = assayde. Cf. *Florence of Rome* (397) :

"And sye the garsons assay þer stedys";
also, *Eglam* (1191):
"He rode a course to assay his stede."
Cf. Sc. say = assay.

31/1003. The chýlde spákke to.

32/1009-10. G. The empęrōur saydę and wax all pālę, 'Sonę, whȳ umbraydest mē of bālę?'

32/1009-14. G. changes the order to 1012-14 following 1008, then 1009-11, which improves the sense.

32/1012. G. [right] joyfull.

32/1013. *wyth* = into the presence of.

32/1024. G. of Segramõūr. Possibly the scribe momentarily confused the name with *Sir Eglamour*, which he had already copied often in the romance of that name.

32/1031. *vsed by* = familiar or well known in? The general sense is clear.

32/1032. The relative *which* seems to be omitted. In connection with the name *Egare*, *Sir Degarre* has an interesting explanation in regard to the hermit's christening of the child:

"He hit nemnede Degarre:
Degarre nowt elles ne is
But thing that not neuer whar hit is,
O the thing that is negth forlorn al so,
For thi the schild he nemnede thous tho."—(252-256.)

Evidently Emaré had some such thought in mind when she changed her name to Egaré.

GLOSSARIAL INDEX.

A, *interj.* 25/787, ah.
A, *pron.* (?) 31/989, he.
A-bowe, *v. refl.* 31/981, bow.
A-cyse, *n.* 26/830, a-syse, 29/912, manner; asyce, 24/748, estate. Cf. N. E. D. *Assize*, 8.
A-ferd, *adj.* 11/321; aferde, 21/655, a-ferde, 22/698, afraid.
A-fyne, *adv.* 29/913, finally; and fyne, 19/580, probably a corruption of the same. Fr. *à fin.*
A-gayn, A-gayne. *See* A-ȝeyn.
A-lyȝte,*v. pret.*32/1018, dismounted.
Amerayle, *n.* 4/109, emir; amerayles, 6/159.
Anamered, *v. pret.* 31/997 (of), was charmed with; an-amered, *pp.* 13/400 (of), anamored, 8/226 (tylle), enamoured. Cf. N. E. D. *Enamoured.*
And, *conj.* 32/1011, 1012, if.
Anker, *n.* 9/275, anchor.
A-non, *adv.* 14/442, 27/860, 28/886; a-none, 25/777, presently, soon.
A-qweynte, *v. refl.* 30/965, become acquainted with.
Arunde, 1/8, errand, message.
A-ryce, *v.* 9/260, arise, begin.
Asowr, *n.* 4/113, azure.
Asyce, Asyse. *See* A-cyse.
A-ventowres, *n.* 24/754, adventures.
A-ȝeyn, *prep.* 7/203, 24/752, 29/932, 31/986, 32/1016, towards; 7/206, opposite; 31/974, on the occasion of; 10/295, contrary to; *adv.* 10/309, 28/890, 29/910, again. A-gayn, *prep. postpos.* 11/317, against; a-ȝayne, *adv.* 15/455, again; a-ȝayn, *prep.* 30/971, towards.

Bale, *n.* 32/1010, sorrow.
Be, *prep.* 25/787, by.
Beere, *n.* 17/539, bear.

Be-ȝeten, *pp.* 2/44, begotten.
Be-lafte, *v. pret.* 15/472; by-laft, 16/496, remained.
Be-refe, *v. tr.* 25/801, deprive of; *pret.* be-rafte, 19/582; by-rafte, 25/803.
Be-sette, *pp.* 16/482, attacked, surrounded.
Be-stadde, *pp.* 11/334, 22/682, bestead.
Be-þowght, *v. refl. pret.* 9/280 = [vm]-beþowght, reflected. *See note.*
Be-tydde, *v.* 9/253, be-tyde, 30/970, happen.
Ble, *n.* 9/270, 19/590, 21/644, colour
Blo, *adj.* 11/318, dark, *here applied to a stormy sea.*
Blode, *n.* 3/73, 16/513, 20/635, race, lineage.
Body, *n.* 28/897, creature. Cf. N. E. D. 111, 13, *for early quotations.*
Bote, *n.* 32/1011, help.
Bour, *n.* 23/730; bowre, 3/63, 23/740, 28/899; bowres, 24/755, 27/873; bowrys, 2/28, bower, lady's chamber.
Brede, *n.* 19/581, 29/914, roast meat.
Brente, *v. pret.* 17/533; *pp.* 25/796, burned.
Bryddes, *n.* 6/166, birds.
Brym, *n.* 12/349; brymme, 22/694, shore.
Bullus, *n.* 8/239, papal bull.
Burgeys, *n.* 26/839, 28/886, 888, 895, burgess.
By, *prep.* 10/294, along.
Byddynge, *n.* 24/768, command.
By-forn, *prep.* 6/163, before.
Byggynge, *n.* 23/709, dwelling.
By-laft. *See* Be-lafte.
By-rafte. *See* Be-refe.

EMARÉ. E

Glossarial Index.

Carbunkulle, *n.* carbuncle, 5/127.
Carefulle, *adj.* 11/328, full of care; karefulle, 22/676, 26/808.
Case, *n.* 19/605, chance; kase, 21/647.
Certys, *adv.* 28/880, certainly; sērtes, 19/605.
Chalange, *n.* 27/851 (to), fault. Cf. N. E. D. *Challenge, sb.* 3.
Chare, *n.* 7/201, travelling-carriage.
Chawnses, *n.* (ylle), 22/684, misfortunes.
Chere, *n.* 7/214, 10/300, 25/807, frame of mind (cf. N. E. D. *Cheer*, 2 and 3); 28/892, 31/999, face.
Chynne, *n.* 29/924, chin (synecdoche for face).
Clere, *adj.* 5/128, 8/234, 24/742, 26/810, beautiful.
Clypte, *v. pret.* 32/1020, embraced; klypped, 7/212.
Crapawtes, *n.* 5/142, toad-stones; crapowtes, 4/94. Cf. N. E. D. *Crapaud, Crapautee.*
Crystalle, *n.* 6/155, crystal.
Crystendom, *n.* 14/428, christendom.
Crystyante, *n.* 4/108, 20/635, 30/969, christendom.
Cumbered, *pp.* 16/483, oppressed.
Curtays, *adj.* 2/36, 40, 3/64, 27/850; curteys, 3/74, 23/724, 738, 27/850, 872, courteous.
Curtesye, *n.* 3/58, 14/425, good manners.
Curteysly(e), *adv.* 27/868, 28/894, mannerly, with good manners.

Deamondes, *n.* 5/130, deamoundes, 6/153, diamonds.
Dede, *v. pret.* 9/269, put.
Dele, *n.* 12/356, sorrow; 20/613, lamentation.
Dele, *v. tr.* 1/3, 2/42, 26/826, distribute.
De[l]fulle, *adj.* 19/606, doleful. *See note.*
Delycyus, *adj.* 12/370, delicious.
Deuylle, *n.* 17/536, devil.
Do. *See* ᵭo.
Dolys, *n.* 26/826, alms.
Dome, *n.* 31/984, judgment.
Dowbylle, *adj.* 16/504, double.
Dragon, *n.* 17/539.
Drowȝ, *v. pret.* 26/832, drew.
Drury, *adj.* 26/808, dreary.

Dwelle, *v.* 1/19, dwelles, 23/721: *pret.* dwelled, 9/274, 11/325, 19/577, 21/673, remained; 11/340, 22/686, dwelled.
Dyght, *v. tr.* 2/42, ordain, govern, prepare, arrange; dyghte, 1/3; *pret.* dyght, 26/830; dyȝte, 7/193; dyȝth, 26/826; *pp.* dyght, 4/88, 5/133, 137, 6/177, 10/285, 14/440, 23/717; dyȝt, 19/578; dyȝth, 15/458; y-dyȝth, 13/395.

Ellys, *adv.* 4/105, else.
Emerawdes, *n.* 5/152, emeralds.
Erdly, *adj.* 13/396, earthly; erdyly, 22/701; erþely, 8/245.
Eyer, *n.* 22/690, air; eyr, 11/346.

Fare, *v.* 7/195, go.
Fay, *n.* 10/296, faith.
Fayry, *n.* 4/104, magic contrivance. Cf. N. E. D. *Fairy*, A. 3.
Fee, *n.* 22/686, property.
Fele, *adj.* 26/823, many.
Felle, *n.* 10/306, skin.
Feltred, *adj.* 17/540, with matted hair. Cf. N. E. D. *Feltered.*
Fende, *n.* 14/446, 17/540, 18/563, fiend.
Fere, *n.* 7/215 (in), 8/237 (yn), in company, together.
Ferly, *n.* 12/351, wonder.
Fleted, *v. pret.* 10/313, 21/650, drifted.
Fode, *n.* 16/507, nurseling, *i. e.* child.
Folde, *v. tr.* 29/939, embrace.
Fome, *n.* 16/497, 25/805, 26/818, foam; 26/835 (synecdoche for sea).
For-bere, *v.* 20/611 (of), forbear.
For-lorne, *pp.* 9/255, lost, here damned.
Fre, *adj.* 1/10, 22, 3/71, 8/247, 10/308, 25/792, 26/831, 27/844, 28/884, 30/963, 31/979, 32/1013, of gentle birth and breeding. Cf. N. E. D. *Free*, I, 3.
Frely, *adj.* 16/507, 29/939, *a synonym of the preceding.*
Fro, *prep.* 2/53, 17/532, 24/744, 25/776, from.
Fryght, *n.* 19/600, frith, *i. e.* enclosed land (field or forest); frythes, 2/29.
Fydylleyng, *n.* 13/390, fiddling.

Glossarial Index. 51

Fyne. See A-fyne.

Game, n. 15/474, pleasure ; 28/874, jest.
Gare, n. 7/198, gore (synecdoche for gown) ; gore, 29/938.
Garnettes, n. 6/156, garnets.
Gate, n. 26/828, way.
Gay, adj. 14/444, beautiful.
Gedered, v. tr. pret. 16/488, gathered.
Gent, adj. 2/55, 7/191, 13/403, 29/932, 32/1016, gentle.
Gentelle, adj. 14/441, noble-looking (?) ; gentylle, 3/73, 16/513, 20/635, noble, high-born ; gentylle, 13/391, noble-looking (?).
Gle, n. 5/132, music ; 15/474, joy.
Glysteryng, adj. 4/100, 12/350, 22/699, glittering.
Godele, adj. 16/503 ; godely, 87/198, goodly.
Gore. See Gare.
Grete ende, 28/905, 29/917, thumb (?). See note on l. 905.
Grette, v. 18/556, 24/772, wept.
Growht, v. pret.21/669, lamented (?). See note.
Gruf, adj. 21/656, face downwards.
Gryght, n. 19/597 = O.E. grið, protection.

Haluendelle, adv. 14/444, half.
Happes, n. 21/651, fortunes.
Harpe, n. 13/390.
Hele, n. 18/570, health.
Hende, adj. 3/84 (used substantively), courteous ; adv. 17/537, near.
Hette, v. pres. 22/703, 704, are called, am called ; pret. 2/34, 12/360 ; pret. hyght, 11/342, 28/879 ; hyȝte, 3/85, 7/199 ; or pres. (?) hyȝth, 11/338 ; pres. 28/876.
Heþennes, n. 4/109, heathendom.
Hode, n. 31/992, hood.
Honeste, adj. 13/386, honourable, fitting.
Horn, n. 6/165.
Hye, adj. 6/165, high.
Hye, n. 7/193 (in), haste ; 4/103, hygh (on).
Hyght. See Hette.
Hynþur, adj. 21/654, hinder.
Hyȝynge, n. 16/511 (yn), haste.
Hyȝte, hyȝth. See Hette.

Inne, n. 30/960, inn ; yn, 26/839.
Ire, n. 15/455, anger.

Jwelle, n. 4/107, jewel.

Karefulle. See Carefulle.
Kase. See Case.
Kassydonys, n. 5/128, chalcedony.
Kaytyf, n. 10/293, caitiff.
Kelle, n. 10/303, hair-net.
Kessed, v. pret. 31/995, kissed.
Keuered, pp. 12/374, 25/784, 30/945, recovered ; kouered, 10/289.
Klypped. See Clypte.
Knyȝtus, n. 5/151. See note.
Konnyngest, adj. 14/427, most skilful.
Koralle, n. 6/154, coral.
Kouered. See Keuered.
Kowrs, n. 27/867, course (of a meal).
Kowth, v. pret. 2/42 ; kowþe, 2/54, 21/672, 23/737 ; kowȝþe, 13/382, could.
Kurtulle, n. 13/392, kirtle, underrobe ; kurtylle, 27/848.
Kygh, n. 19/594 = kith, i.e. native land. Cf. N. E. D. Kith, 3.
Kyngus marke, 16/504, birth-mark signifying royalty.

Lappes, n. 21/654, folds. Cf. N. E. D. Lap.
Lasshed, v. pret. 10/298, fell in showers.
Lay, n. 10/295, law.
Layes, n. 32/1030, lays, songs.
Le, n. 11/348 (of), 26/834 (on). See Lythe.
Leede, n. 22/702, people (yn = among).
Lees, n. 4/110, falsehood.
Lende, v. 17/515, arrive.
Lene, adj. 12/365, lean.
Lent, pp. 13/404, bestowed.
Lere, n. 10/294, cheeks, face.
Lesynge, n. 28/880, falsehood.
Lette, v. 20/618, stop.
Lettynge, n. 27/843, impediment, delay.
Lor, n. 25/792, lord.
Lorde, n. used as interj.30/940, Lord.
Loþly, adj. 18/563, hateful.
Lufsumme, adj. 27/864, lovable.
Lust, n. 26/833, wish.

Lyflope, *n.* 25/803, means of support.
Lylye, *n.* 3/66, 7/205, lily
Lyne, *n.* 27/864, linen.
Lyon, *n.* 17/539, lion.
Lythe, *adj.* 11/348, 26/834, pleasant, combined with le (cf. N. E. D. Lee, especially I, 1, 2, 3) calm. *But also, see note on l.* 348.
Ly3te, *v. pret.* 7/206, 210, dismounted.

Madde, *adj.*, 11/335, 22/683, insane.
Mangery, *n.* 15/469, feast.
Marke, *v.* 12/376, mark, *i. e.* paint, embroider, *or perhaps* mark for embroidering; marked, *pp.* showing marks of.
Maystrye, *n.* 6/174, power.
Menske, *n.* 3/69, respect, dignity.
Menstralle, *n.* 15/468, minstrel; menstrelles, 1/13, 11/319; men[s]trelles, 27/867; menstrellys, 5/132.
Menstralse, *n.* 13/388, minstrelsy.
Mete, *n.* 7/218, 13/401, 23/722, food.
Meteles, *adj.* 12/355, 364, 23/718, without food.
Metewhyle, *n.* 8/229, 13/406, meal.
Moch. *See* Myche.
Molde, *n.* 8/246, mould, earth.
Mone, *n.* 10/314, lamentation.
Moo, *adj.* 3/60, more.
Mornede, *v. pret.* 23/732, mourned.
Mornyng, *n.* 1/21, mourning; 20/626, mornynge.
Mot, *v.* 25/775, must.
Myche, *adj.* 3/78, 4/92, 5/140, 13/388, 15/463, 16/485, 20/637, 21/668; mychyl, 3/69; mychylle, 5/131; mykelle, 28/885; mykylle, 1/20, 11/341, 24/747, 749, 26/892; mykulle, 31/987; moch, 15/43, much.
Myn, *adj.* 29/915, less.
Mynge, *v.* 29/926, remind, tell.
Myrght, *n.* 1/20, mirth.
Myswrowht, *pp.* 9/281, done amiss.

Nakette, *n.* 4/94, 5/142, a precious stone. Agate? *See note.*
Nām, *v. pret.* 12/368, took.
Ner, *v. pret.* 10/297, were not.
Nome, *n.* 2/27, name.
Nortur, *n.* 3/62, nortowre, 23/731, good manners.

Norysse, *n.* 7/199, nurse.

Onus, *adv.* 21/664, once.
Onyx, *n.* 5/128.
Ordeyne, *v. tr.* 26/823, equip, prepare.
Ore, *n.* 9/275, 26/832, oar.
Owth, *v.* 21/667, ought.

Palle, *n.* 27/848, pall, fine cloth. Cf. N. E. D. *Pall*, I, 1.
Pappe, *n.* 21/663, breast; pappes, 21/657.
Paym, *n.* 19/595, penalty.
Perydotes, *n. plur.* 6/155, greenish chrysolite. (O.Fr. *peridot, peridon, pelidor,* derivation uncertain.)
Place, *n.* 16/499, 25/788 (yn), in the course of experience? *See note on l.* 499.
Play, *v. refl.* 6/183, 11/345, 22/689, amuse one's self; 9/254, have sexual intercourse.
Playnge, *vb. n.* 3/78. *See* Play.
Pope, *n.* 8/233, 30/956; Popus, 8/239.
Powste, *n.* 26/837, power.
Poyn, *n.* 12/357, yn poyn[t] to, at the point of.
Prese, *n.* 15/464, crowd.
Price, *n.* 26/829, pryce, 9/259, prys, 16/485, pryse, 24/749, 31/985, renown; prys, 4/92, pryse, 5/131, 140, value.
Prike, *v. tr.* 23/737, spur.
Purnyance, *n.* 15/458, provision.
Pyght, *pp.* 4/89, set.

Rappes, *n.* 21/660, blows.
Ray(e), *n.* 14/415, striped cloth; 14/430, 15/451, *the same, or rei =* king? *See note.*
Remeueth, *v.* 7/187, departs.
Resseyned, *pp.* 17/517, 19/578, received.
Romans, *n.* 7/216, romance (French?).
Rubyes, *n.* 4/91, 5/130, 139, rubies.
Ryche, *adj.* 3/80, 82, 4/100, 107, 113, 14/415, 430, 15/451, 468, 19/590, 21/644, 22/686, 27/848, 28/912, splendid.
Ryghtwes, *adj.* 1/17, righteous.

Saf, *conj.* 25/779, save, *i.e.* except (it be).
Safere, *n.* 5/127, sapphire.

Glossarial Index. 53

Sale, n. 3/62, 15/459, hall.
Sawe, n. 11/319, story.
Sawtre, n. 13/389, psaltery.
See-fome, n. 25/805, sea-foam.
Sembelant, n. 8/220, appearance.
Semely, adj. 1/9, 2/32, 48, 4/93, 5/135, 141, 6/171, 14/423, 15/459, 471, 16/486, 501, 30/942, fair, seemly.
Senatowres, n. 5/152. See note on l. 151.
Serke, n. 16/501, smock.
Sertes. See Certys.
Seuen-ny3th, n. 11/326; seuene nyght, 21/674, week.
Shate, v. tr. pret. 9/273, pushed.
Shene, adj. 5/150, 16/489, 29/933, shining.
Shente, pp. 20/628, ruined.
Shypmen, n. 26/829, sailors.
Shoope, v. tr. pret. 1/2, created.
Shylynge, n. 17/524, shilling.
Shype, n. 20/638, to shype=aboard.
Slye, adj. 3/67, skilful.
Smalle, adj. 13/391, slender.
Snelle, adv. 10/309, quickly.
Sond, n. 11/332, dispensation.
Sond(e), n. 1/18, 12/352, 20/645, sand.
Sowdan, n. 6/158, 170, 173, sultan.
Sowened, v. pret. 21/645, 25/780, 29/935, swooned.
Sowenynge, n. 10/284, 18/551; sownyng, 10/289; swonynge, 19/608; swooning.
Specyally, adv. 28/900, specially.
Specyalte, n. 6/176, in specyalte, as a special gift.
Spedde, pp. 17/519, prospered.
Spendyng, n. 9/271, 19/592, money to spend.
Sprynge, v. 9/256, be spread abroad.
Spycerye, n. 27/853, 28/891, the sweet course.
S[t]ayde (?), v. tr. pret. 31/1000, reined in? But see note on l. 1000.
Stede, n. 12/372, place.
Stounde, n. 1/19, while.
Stronge, adj. 21/665, rough.
Stuffed, pp. 6/168, thickly crowded.
Stye, n. 7/196, 17/543, path.
Stynte, v. 10/302; tr. 26/815, stop.
Surkote, n. 21/652, surcoat, upper dress.
Swayne, n. 13/384, countryman.
Swyde, adv. 7/219, swyþe, 8/242, quickly.

Sy, v. tr. pret. 27/869; sye, 3/68, sy3, 13/398: sy3en, 10/299, saw.
Syche, adj. 20/626, such.
Sygh, adv. 18/560=syþe, afterwards.
Sykyng, n. 11/328, 22/676; sykynges, 26/809, sighing.
Sympulle, adj. 20/632, of humble origin.
Syþe, n. 22/692, side.
Syþe, n. 8/225, time. Ofte siþe, often.

Tabours, n. 13/389, drums.
Take, v. tr. pret. 29/920, give; toke, 18/547; toke hem be-twene, 25/799, decided.
Takulle, n. 26/830, tackle.
Tane, v. tr. 22/690, take.
Taw3te, v. tr. pret. 3/61, 12/376, 23/731; thaw3th, 3/58; thaw3te, 31/973, taught.
Tene, n. 16/483, distress.
Testymonyeth, v. 32/1029; testimoyeth, 6/162, testifies.
Thaw3th. See Taw3te.
The, v. 25/775, thrive.
Thewe, n. 3/58, behaviour.
Tho, prep. 17/528, to.
Þo, adv. 29/926, 30/956, 32/1018; þoo, 2/51, 28/885; do, 17/533, then.
Þonge, v. pret. 21/659=dong, struck.
Þowht, v. pret. 12/356; þow3t[e], 30/951, 955, þow3th, 8/227, 22/700, thought.
Þow3t(h), n. 8/223, 227, 17/530, thought.
Þow3tur, n. 8/226, 14/422; þow3þur, 32/1008, daughter.
Þrynge, v. 10/304, throng.
Thylle. See Tylle.
Þyng(e), n. plur. 2/41, 3/64, 75, 11/333, 12/379, 13/382, 15/466, 18/560, 22/681, 23/712, 724, 24/762, 27/852, 30/964, 31/976, things.
Topase, n. 5/139, topaze, 4/91, topaz.
Tre, n. 12/365, staff or stick; 21/656, probably, thwart. See note on l. 365.
Trewe-loué-flour, n. 5/125. 149, Herb Paris. See note on l. 125.
Trommpus, n. 13/389, trumpets.
Trone, n. 1/1, 22/680, 26/820, 836, throne.
Tyde, n. 16/487, 22/691, 31/993, time.

54   Glossarial Index.

Tylle, prep. postpos. 8/226, 13/411, 28/895, 902, to ; conj. 18/545, 570, thylle, 16/502, until.

Valed, v. pret. 31/992, doffed, pushed down.
Vanyte, n. 4/105, illusion.
Verament, adv. 14/433, 20/619, truly.
Vertues, n. 5/152, magic powers.
Vmbraydest, v. tr. 29/929, 32/1010, upbraidest.
Vnhende, adj. 14/445, discourteous; 17/534, 25/794, evil.
Vnsemely, adj. 21/660, rude.
Vnykorn, n. 6/164, unicorn.
Vseden¹, v. pret. 3/62, practised ; pp. vsed, 32/1031, familiar.
Vyce, n. 24/742 ; Vysage, n. 21/653, face.

Wan, v. tr. pret. 6/173, won.
Wanne, adj. 24/771, wan.
Warye, v. tr. 21/667, curse.
Wawe, n. 11/322 ; wawes, 21/658, wave.
Wax, v. pret. 23/728, 24/771, 32/1009, grew ; woxen, 30/950.
Weddewede, n. 3/77 (yn), widowhood, i.e. as a widower.
Wede, n. 8/250, 12/366, 14/447, 20/612, 22/699, 23/736, 31/988, dress.
Wedur, n. 11/348, weather; wederus, 11/336 ; weþur, 26/834.
Wele, n. 26/824, wealth.
Welle-a-wey, interj. 26/812, alas.
Wende, v. 3/81, 6/184, 17/514, 531, go.
Wene, n. 5/153, doubt.
Wesh, v. pret. 7/218, washed: w(h)esshen, 28/890 ; wysh, 27/866.
Whales bone, 2/33, walrus-ivory. See note.
Wolde, n. 13/399, power.
Wone, v. 1/5, 32/1034, dwell; woned, 26/840.

Woo, n. 11/324, 336, 18/555, 20/621, 637, 21/648, 22/684, 28/882, 29/925 ; wo, 18/573, 24/763.
Worche, v. tr. 8/227, work, do.
Wordes, n. 26/824, world's. See note.
Wordy, adj. 8/250, 12/366, 14/447; worþy, 20/612, 23/736, 31/988, worthy.
Wordyly, adv. 3/83, worthily.
Worshyp, n. 30/966, honour.
Worth, v. 21/648, 22/684, come upon (wo ... worth).
Wote, v. tr. pres. indic. 9/269, knows; pret. wyste, 19/579 ; infin. wyte, 5/153, 14/435.
Wryng, v. 28/881, force their way.
Wyght, n. 22/701, being.
Wyght, adj. 2/39, brave.
Wynne, v. tr. 30/957, wynnen, 26/827, win.
Wysh. See Wesh.

ʒaf hem ylle, 25/778, lamented.
ʒarked, v. 11/329, 22/677 (ʒore), prepared ready, i.e. ordained. See note.
Y-dyʒth. See Dyght.
ʒede, v. pret. 7/213, 215, went ; ʒode, 17/516.
Ylke, adj. 4/114, 6/166, each ; 24/770, same.
Ymagerye, n. 6/168, figures.
ʒode. See ʒede.
ʒonge. See ʒynge.
ʒoo, adv. 28/888, yea.
ʒore, adv. 11/329, 22/677, ready. See ʒarked.
Yrpe, n. 10/285, earth.
Y-wysse, adv. 28/906, certainly.
Yʒen, n. 10/297, eyes.
ʒyf, conj. 20/616, 31/980, if.
ʒynge, adj. 2/41, 3/65 10/301, 305, 12/380, 18/569, 20/610, 23/710, 725, young ; ʒonge, 22/707.

INDEX OF NAMES.

Abro, 2/57, 3/61, 7/199, Abra.
Amadas, 5/122.
Artyus, 2/27, 37, Arthur.
Babylone, 6/158.
Blawncheflour, 5/146.
Brytayne, 32/1030.
Cesyle, 3/80, 6/181, Sicily.
Egare, 12/360, 24/761, 29/908, 923, 32/1007; Egarye, 14/437, 22/704, 26/810, 32/1007, 1032.
Emare, 1/23, 2/47, 27/841, 29/907, 922, 30/952, 961, 31/973, 982, 32/1006, 1023; Emarye, 26/840.
Erayne, 2/34.
Florys, 5/146.
France, 16/481.

Galys, 11/338, 16/484, 487, 24/743, 746, 29/909, 30/967, 31/986.
Isowde, 5/134.
Iurdan, 22/687.
Kadore, 11/342, 12/361, 13/385, 409, 14/416, 421, 16/490, 508, 24/758, 25/775, 30/940; Kodore, 24/751.
Rome, 8/233, 238, 22/679, 30/959.
Sareȝyne, 16/482.
Segramour, 16/506; Segramowre, 23/739, 31/995, 31/1000; Segramowres, 28/876; [S]egramour, 32/1024.
Tergaunte, 3/85.
Trystram, 5/134.
Ydoyne, 5/122.

The manufacturer's authorised representative in the EU for product
safety is Oxford University Press España S.A. of El Parque Empresarial
San Fernando de Henares, Avenida de Castilla, 2 - 28830 Madrid
(www.oup.es/en or product.safety@oup.com). OUP España S.A. also acts
as importer into Spain of products made by the manufacturer.
Printed and bound by CPI Group (UK) Ltd, Croydon, CR0 4YY

22/04/2026

02094916-0007